SUCCEEDING IN EXAMS
& ASSESSMENTS

INSIDE TRACK

SUCCEEDING IN EXAMS & ASSESSMENTS

Dr Eddie Blass

School of Education,
University of Hertfordshire

PEARSON
Longman

Harlow, England • London • New York • Boston • San Francisco • Toronto
Sydney • Tokyo • Singapore • Hong Kong • Seoul • Taipei • New Delhi
Cape Town • Madrid • Mexico City • Amsterdam • Munich • Paris • Milan

I wish to dedicate this book to my parents who never gave up on my endless years of study and career changes, and have supported and encouraged me all the way to and through my Doctorate. I think I have finally settled where I belong.

Pearson Education Limited

Edinburgh Gate
Harlow
Essex CM20 2JE
England

and Associated Companies throughout the world

Visit us on the World Wide Web at:
www.pearsoned.co.uk

First published 2009

ISBN: 978-0-273-72172-7

British Library Cataloguing-in-Publication Data
A catalogue record for this book is available from the British Library

Library of Congress Cataloging-in-Publication Data
A catalogue record for this book is available from the Library of Congress

10 9 8 7 6 5 4 3 2 1
13 12 11 10 09

Typeset in 9/13 pt Helvetica Neue by 3
Printed and bound in Great Britain by Henry Ling Ltd, at the Dorset Press Dorchester, Dorset

The publisher's policy is to use paper manufactured from sustainable forests.

BRIEF CONTENTS

CONTENTS

Contents

Contents

Contents

ABOUT THE AUTHOR

Dr Eddie Blass went to Quintin Kynaston School, a large comprehensive school in inner London, and studied for her first degree at what was Oxford Polytechnic. She left with a 2:2 having not really enjoyed the 'university experience'. Her career in industry moved her into a training role, and from there she decided to go into teaching. Having taught in schools, Further Education colleges, and Higher Education, Eddie realised why she had not done so well herself at university, and this book is her guide to helping students make the transition from school into Higher Education. Eddie completed her Doctorate in Education at Durham University and is now based in the School of Education at the University of Hertfordshire.

A PERSONAL NOTE AS AN INTRODUCTION

This book is aimed at all new students in the university sector regardless of the course of study they are choosing. It helps students make the transition from school to university teaching and learning, and/or helps people returning to studying from time out in the workplace get to grips with the learning skills they will need to succeed at university – and then demonstrates how these skills can also be employed in the workplace.

This is a book for students – not parents, academics, teachers or concerned friends. It is a personal guide for the student themself. The book will be relevant to all courses in the arts, liberal arts, social sciences, business studies, education and humanities. The author is unclear of its use to medical students and scientists who are involved in laboratory work rather than the lecture–exam cycle.

This book is written by someone who was never a good student – and it wasn't from lack of trying! In fact you could argue that it is written by someone who was a very good student – they just didn't end up with a good degree. Perhaps it was my arrogance and my self-belief that kept me going, but having 'only' achieved a 2:2 in my first degree at Oxford Polytechnic, I felt I wanted to prove I was 'better' than that. Hence I scraped through my Masters degree, again struggling with the exams, and then went on to complete a Doctorate in Education at Durham University. Finally I felt I had proved to myself that I could do it – whatever 'it' is.

When I was at school I always wanted to be a lawyer. I went to a very large, inner city comprehensive school in London at the time when the Inner London Education Authority was being disbanded. Not that the history mattered, but suffice to say I ended up studying for my three different A levels at three different local schools – travelling from one to another between classes. I left school with A level grades B, D and E – and was the top girl for that year in my base school. I'm not telling you this as a sob-story, I'm telling you because you might be thinking that your past performance is going to shape your future. It isn't. If I could leave school with bad A levels and ultimately end up with a Doctorate then anyone can.

Also, don't think it is all about memory. The reason I never pursued the law was because the law exams are famously dependent on memory – and mine isn't good. You need to remember statutes, cases, years, etc. for law exams, which seems stupid really when you can look them up on a daily basis once you've qualified as a lawyer. However, there is an old adage that the proof of the pudding is in the eating, so to test out my own ideas on how to pass exams, I went back to the Open

University to study for an undergraduate law degree, and guess what – I passed the exams, and gained another degree!

So where did my insight into how to pass exams come from?

Having started my career in HRM in industry, I gradually specialised in training and development, and then decided to go into teaching. I hated school, so I have no idea what made me think I'd like it better as a teacher, and I didn't. Hence I moved on to teach in FE colleges, and then went into university lecturing. This is where my world changed. Suddenly I had to mark examination scripts – and I could see exactly why people failed!

I guess the insight in this book therefore comes from having put in lots of effort as a student and not done well, and then seeing it from the other side – the markers' view – and knowing where I went wrong. I have a deep wish now that someone had taught me what I've learnt from marking before I ever sat any exams. I know I would have done better. Hence this book is my attempt at passing on this knowledge to you in the hope that it allows you to do better than you might otherwise. I know it helped numerous students at the university where I used to teach, as their exam scores improved and overall standards on the HR courses rose.

Passing the exam is only part of the game though, there are other tricks to doing well in Higher Education, like how to 'read' effectively, and how to use a 'model'. Again most of these skills are assumed as present when you start studying but the reality for most of us is they are not. These are not ideas that you are taught at school, but you need them from day one at university. This book, therefore, covers the study skills necessary to help you prepare for exams as well as the techniques needed to actually pass them.

ACKNOWLEDGEMENTS

Thank you to all the fantastic colleagues I have worked with at the University of Hertfordshire, University of Derby, Ashridge and Dearne Valley Business School. In particular, thanks to Dr Ann Davis who is currently at Aston University – without her support I would never have survived the early years.

PUBLISHER'S ACKNOWLEDGEMENTS

We are grateful to the following for permission to reproduce copyright material:

Table 7.1 adapted from *Motivating Humans*, Sage Publications (Ford, M. E. 1992) p. 220.

In some instances we have been unable to trace the owners of copyright material, and we would appreciate any information that would enable us to do so.

1 ▶ HOW TO USE A MODEL

This chapter looks at the 'traditions' associated with universities in terms of the language that is often used, the nature of the university itself, and the concept of 'reading'. It helps you think about what you personally want to achieve while at university, and how well the university experience can help you achieve these aims.

This chapter will cover:

- The purpose of studying at university
- Some of the language that is unique to a university setting
- How to get started with reading

USING THIS CHAPTER

INTRODUCTION

In this chapter I try to demystify some of the language you hear in academic circles, and help you make sense of what some of your lecturers might be saying. Some academics deliberately use language that is inaccessible to students – the word 'inaccessible' in this context is a good example. How can language be 'inaccessible'? You don't need to go through a language to gain access to somewhere so what does 'inaccessible' mean in this context? If language is 'inaccessible', then it is being expressed in a way that makes it difficult for everyone to understand. It is a form of jargon that is used in academic circles, and only understood by other academics. This does not need to be the case. At undergraduate and postgraduate levels, everyone should be able to understand what is being said, and hence this chapter tries to make such inaccessible language understandable by everyone.

There are times, of course, when use of inaccessible academic language is appropriate, and that is another reason why it is important to understand the nuances of the language so that you can understand what it means for day-to-day usage, but also appreciate its subtleties as you progress through the levels of your study all the way to your doctorates. Finally, this chapter introduces you to the theories that underpin the philosophy of a university and why you chose to come, and what you can expect to get out of your time at university.

HAVING AN ARGUMENT

You will often hear academics/lecturers talk about 'having an argument', or 'arguing a particular point'. This does not mean that they have had a falling out and are fighting in the same way that friends and families argue. It means that they are taking a particular line of thought and are arguing that case against a colleague who might be taking a different line of thought. It is more like a court case with the lawyers on the respective sides arguing in front of the jury that their client is right and the other lawyer's client is wrong. In essence, you are the jury.

For example, in the Business Studies subject of Human Resource Management, a class might be reviewing an exercise in which a worker is continually making mistakes at work. The lecturer who teaches Employee Development (training and learning in the workplace) might 'argue' that the worker is making mistakes because they haven't been trained properly and hence they don't know how to do the job. The lecturer who teaches Employee Resourcing (recruitment and selection and workforce planning) might 'argue' that they have recruited the wrong person to do the job. The lecturer who teaches Employee Reward (pay and performance management) might 'argue' that if the employee were only paid for each correct cycle of performance and docked pay for every mistake, they would probably make less mistakes. All three views are completely different, and all three views might be equally correct. So who wins the argument?

Arguments in academic life are not intended to be won. There are no right answers as there is actually very little that we can categorically prove to be right with absolute certainty. Hence an argument is a perspective, or a view that someone is taking, based on the evidence that they have, interpreted in the way that they have chosen to interpret it. One way that academics present their arguments is through models.

WHAT IS A MODEL?

If someone mentioned the word 'model' to you, you'd probably think of a tall, beautiful person, walking down a catwalk, modelling clothes in a fashion show. Alternatively, you might think of an airfix model or model car that you had as a child which you painstakingly put together with glue. Others might be thinking of a scale model of a building, or a model village such as Legoland. I suspect none of you would be thinking about a diagram drawn on a page in a textbook – but that is what an academic model is.

In academic terms, a model is a representation of what someone has done with some data. Let's take laundry as an example to explain the principle.

At the end of the week you go home and tip all your dirty clothes out on to the floor. What do you have? A big pile of underwear, trousers, t-shirts, jumpers, and so forth.

What do you do with them? You don't put them all in the washing machine together as some clothes need to go at lower temperatures than others, some colours may run, and some items take longer in the wash than others. So, you sort them out into various piles of washing. You might go for hot wash, cold wash and quick wash.

hot wash   cold wash   quick wash

Or it may be more appropriate for you to do white wash, coloured wash, hand wash.

white wash   coloured wash   hand wash

It doesn't really matter what you do with them, the point is that you sort them out. This is basically what a model is – the sorting out of laundry. If you think of your laundry as pieces of data, then you are arranging your data into different categories. If someone then gave you another piece of data or laundry, you would be able to predict which category that piece of data or laundry would go into. For example, if you were passed a white t-shirt, it would go in the white wash according to the second categorisation of laundry, or in the hot wash according to the first categorisation.

Hence we now have two models for how we are going to do our laundry: hot wash, cold wash and quick wash; and white wash, coloured wash and hand wash. Once we have done the laundry and the clothes are dry and ready to put away, will you put them in your wardrobe in the same order that you put them in the washing machine? Probably not. Now we will re-categorise the clothes according to their usage, for example casual wear, work wear and accessories, or maybe trousers, tops and underwear. Hence we have two more models for the same set of laundry, giving us four models in total, two for dirty laundry and two for clean laundry, but all using the same pile of clothes as the data.

DRAWING A MODEL

These models could be represented in a number of ways diagrammatically to show the thought patterns on how the data has been arranged. You could have concentric rings with the laundry in the middle, the means of sorting it when dirty on the inside and then the means of sorting it when clean on the outside. This would look something like Figure 1.1.

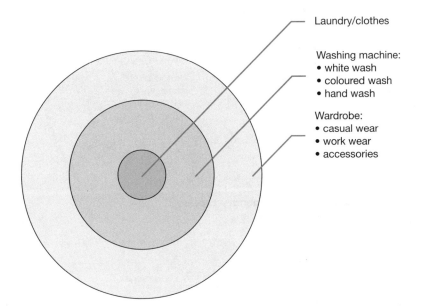

Laundry/clothes

Washing machine:
• white wash
• coloured wash
• hand wash

Wardrobe:
• casual wear
• work wear
• accessories

Figure 1.1 **Concentric ring model of laundry from washing bin to wardrobe**

The concentric ring model represents the dirty clothes as being the central element with the wardrobe as the ultimate arrangement, and you could work from the outside in, i.e. you have your wardrobe full of clothes which move into the washing machine as they get worn, and end up as pile of laundry in need of sorting or ironing; or you can work from the inside out, i.e. you have a pile of laundry or clothes which you then sort for the washing machine, and finally put away in your wardrobe.

An alternative graphical representation might want to give some process direction to your thoughts on laundry, adding some motion to the model to show that one arrangement follows another. In Figure 1.2 you clearly start with the small cog of the laundry which turns the middle cog of the washing machine, driving the larger cog of the wardrobe.

You might feel that both of these models amalgamate too many ideas, and actually you'd like to show how all four data arrangements could be drawn out from the same pile of data/laundry, and hence would come up with something like Figure 1.3.

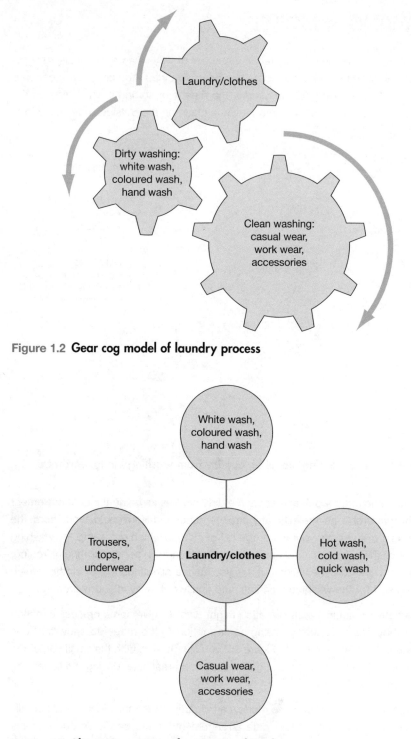

Figure 1.2 **Gear cog model of laundry process**

Figure 1.3 **Alternative means of organising laundry**

All three of the graphical representations are correct and all three show slightly different things. Figure 1.1 shows relationship, in that you can work in from your clean clothes to the dirty clothes which form the basis of laundry. Figure 1.2 shows process, in that the laundry goes into the washing machine to deliver clean clothes. Figure 1.3 shows alternative means of sorting laundry. Which model you choose to present is up to you and would depend on the argument you are trying to make.

USING YOUR MODEL TO SUPPORT AN ARGUMENT

If you want to argue that there are many ways of organising your laundry then you would choose model 3. If you want to argue that clean clothes and dirty clothes are essentially the same things then you would choose model 1. If you want to argue that laundry only becomes clean clothes once it has been through the washing process then you select model 2. So, you can see how data becomes models and models support arguments.

What happens when you have data that doesn't fit into one of the categories? Do you have to scrap your model and come up with another one? Well, you can do. You could alter your model to add another category if you wanted to, or you could identify the data that doesn't fit your model and make this known to the reader as a limitation of your model. For example, one of the limitations of all the models above is that they don't allow for clothes that need to be dry cleaned. Hence if you were presenting your model to a group of students, for example, you would say that one of the limitations of the model is that it doesn't account for dry clean only clothes. You might then argue that you don't see this as detracting from your model as dry clean only clothes are not part of the laundry as such but clothes that need to be taken to a specialist to be cleaned. Hence you might argue that this is not really a limitation as it is outside the boundaries of the data set that you are modelling.

CRITICISING OTHER PEOPLE'S MODELS

Now that you appreciate that a model is simply someone's idea of how to organise their data, you should feel quite confident about criticising their models. After all, you might do it differently. For example, what would happen if you went for the hot wash, cold wash, quick wash model and this resulted in a pair of black trousers going in with white underwear? You'd end up with pink knickers!

When you look at other people's models, or listen to them present an academic argument, always look for the pink knickers. If you can find them, point them out to the person presenting the model as a criticism of the model. They may explain them away as a limitation of the model, which is fine because at least they are acknowledging that they are pink knickers and the model isn't faultless, or they may try to argue that they are not pink knickers – which is often much more fun!

USING OTHER PEOPLE'S MODELS

The whole purpose of an academic producing a model is for other people to use it to help them understand the phenomenon they have been looking at. So, with our laundry example, we would want people to use Figure 1.3, for example, if they had come across a pile of clothes in a room and didn't know what to do with them. We would want them to use the model to consider the best of the four options presented in Figure 1.3 for organising the clothes. Figure 1.3 might be an appropriate model for an au pair or housekeeper in a large family. We would want someone to use Figure 1.2, for example, if they came across a pile of dirty laundry and didn't know what to do with it. Figure 1.2 might be an appropriate model for a laundrette. Figure 1.1 might be more appropriate if you are, for example, the parent of teenagers, trying to get across the relationship between the mess of dirty clothes on the floor and the lack of clothes available for wearing when they want to go out.

As you progress through your studies you will find yourself writing essays and exams. If you can use other people's models in your essays and exams they can help you to argue the point that you want to make as they basically say 'someone else looked at this and this is what they found'. If what they found is in line with your thinking then, great – tell everyone. If what they found is not in line with your thinking then you need to look for the pink knickers in their model so that you can say why it isn't very good and hence discount it.

OTHER NAMES FOR MODELS

At this level of study, the explanation of the model above is enough of a conceptualisation. A conceptualisation is a way of thinking about something. So 'a model' is 'a concept'. As you progress through the academic levels towards your doctorate, you might need to be clearer about how you conceptualise a model compared to other conceptualisations. For example, you might come across 'a framework', or 'a typology', or 'a matrix', or some other title for a diagram. All these diagrams have been conceptualised slightly differently, but the nuance of these differences is not expected to be appreciated at this level of study. For your purposes, they can all be conceptualised as models.

However, having mentioned them, for those of you who are more curious, the differences between them are outlined now, but do not waste energy on this at this point in your studies. A matrix is a way of categorising data according to two elements or axes. A typology is a way of categorising something according to type and they are often represented as hierarchies. A framework is something which guides you in how to look at your data, whereas a model is something which tells you what someone has done with your data. Hence you could argue that Figure 1.3 could be a framework and Figure 1.1 could be a typology. In order to differentiate between the framework, model and typology you would need to know about the methodology applied in deriving the model, and some intention as to how it is to be used. Hopefully this is enough of an explanation to show you why you shouldn't worry about it at the moment but need to be aware of the different terms as they will appear in your textbooks and readings.

NEVER 'DIS' A DISCOURSE

Another word that you might hear academics use in their lectures is 'discourse'. They may talk about a particular discourse in a field, or refer to discourse analysis. So what is a discourse? A discourse is really a perspective, or a view, or an opinion on something that has been named as belonging to a certain school of thought. A 'school of thought' is a shared view held by a number of people in a field when they believe in the same principles, underpinning values, and have the same view of the world. For example, the positivist school of thought believes that something is only true if it can be tested and proven as such, and hence positivists tend to be scientists. Thus a positivist discourse would be that something is only true when it has been tested and proven.

So if it is just an opinion or view, why is it given such a fancy name? This is where the nuances of academic language come into play. In terms of understanding what a discourse is, it is a shared view that can be identified with a named group; in terms of understanding where a discourse comes from, it is established through years of analysis and sharing of research findings in order to find the common view that is to be named and shared. Hence the fancy name of 'discourse' represents the academic effort, debate and analysis which has occurred to establish the view as it is.

As such, if something is presented to you as a discourse, then it is an established opinion in the field, and it needs to be respected as such. It may not be an opinion which you share, but you need to recognise that there is some weight and evidence behind it, and it is a shared opinion among a number of people in the field.

Needless to say, there is usually more than one discourse expressed about any one subject, as different people have different views, and there are many different schools of thought in academia.

PARADIGMS

So how do you differentiate one school of thought from another? This is where the term 'paradigm' comes into play. A paradigm is a value base and set of beliefs that lead to a school of thought. So, for example, a positivist paradigm would be that something needs to be tested in order to be worth noting as it is proven. An interpretivist paradigm, on the other hand, would disagree with this on the basis that if a number of people are interpreting the same thing in the same way then it is worth noting as something is occurring.

There are many different academic paradigms and over time, as you progress through your studies, you may find that you are starting to develop your own way of thinking in line with a particular paradigm. Equally, you may not – and this is not something to worry about. It is not until you embark on your doctoral studies that you need to start situating your work within a paradigm.

At this point in time, all you need to know is that paradigms are the value and belief systems that underpin the different schools of thought, and that each school of thought will have its own discourse.

FROM CRITICISM TO DECONSTRUCTION

When you criticise an idea or model, it is likely that you have seen the pink knickers and you are questioning the way in which the model has been constructed, or put together, from the data that the model's author used. Another way of criticising an argument is to 'deconstruct' it. This literally means pulling it apart. Think of it like a lego building and you deconstruct it back to a pile of lego and then put it all back together again in a 'reconstruction'. Sometimes the new lego building looks different to the original that you pulled apart, while on other occasions you may put it back together again in exactly the same way.

So how do you 'deconstruct' an argument? The basic starting point is to look for the key words in the argument and ask yourself what exactly do those words mean in that argument, and is that a good meaning to give them? To give a very simple example, let's deconstruct the argument 'if you put black trousers in the wash with white underwear you will end up with pink knickers'. You might start off by looking at the concept of black trousers. In this argument the assumption is being made that black trousers will run in the wash, and that they will run with a red dye. How likely is that to be true in your experience? Equally, there is the assumption that the white knickers will pick up the red dye with the result that they appear pink once the washing cycle has finished and they have dried. How likely is that to be true in your experience? Then there is the issue of the wash. If it is a cold wash then it is less likely that the dye will run than if it is a hot wash. Hence the argument is based on a number of factors that may not hold true when deconstructed. Thus a better reconstruction might be 'if you put black trousers that are likely to run, in a hot wash with white underwear that is made of a material that is easy to dye, you may end up with pink knickers'.

ORDINARY WORDS WITH SPECIFIC ACADEMIC MEANING

There are three words in particular that you might use in your everyday conversations that have particular meaning in academic texts and conversations, and you need to be aware of this. These words are valid, reliable and significant.

Significance is a term which has a specific meaning when it is used in relation to measurements of a statistical nature and, because of this, has to be used carefully whenever it refers to results of any kind – even if you haven't used statistics. We use statistics to try to prove something by 'testing a hypothesis'. For example, our hypothesis might be that if we do X then Y occurs. Our test would then be to do X say 100 times and see how many times out of 100 Y occurs. We would then test this statistically to find out if Y occurred enough times for us to be able to conclude that whenever we do X, Y will occur. The significance element is that we can test this to be 95 or 99 per cent sure that when we do X the result will be Y. Therefore if we say that a result is significant, we are saying that we have tested it to be the case such that we are 95 or 99 per cent sure that X results in Y. Once we have done the statistical testing we can say, for example, that X has a significant impact on Y, but until we have done the statistical testing we can only say that X has an impact on Y. If you use the word 'significant' in the same sentence as you talk about results of something or a relationship between elements, then people will expect you to have done the statistics to prove it.

The word valid tends to be used in everyday life to give a shelf life to something, for example a voucher may be valid until a certain date, or a ticket is only valid for certain journeys. In the academic world validity has a much more defined meaning. Something is deemed to be valid if it measures what it says it is going to measure. Hence the term validity is used with regard to whether a study or test actually does what it says it will do. For example, some people would question whether the IQ test is actually a measure of intelligence or a measure of the ability to complete that particular test. Thus some would argue that Mensa membership (only open to those with very high scores in the IQ test) is not a valid measure of intelligence, but rather a valid measure of those able to score highly in the IQ test.

In academia, something is said to be reliable if doing it again would produce the same result, i.e. test and then retest gives the same result. Reliability can be quite a difficult concept to work with. For example, once you have asked someone a question you will have changed them because you will have directed them to think about an issue. How you ask the question will affect the result. If you ask them the same question again, the answer may be different as it will be more considered. Alternatively, if you ask them the same question but in a different manner, the answer may be different. Does this mean the answer is unreliable? In court cases, the opposing side will try to demonstrate that the key witnesses put up by their opponent are unreliable. They will do this by asking the same question in different ways, or asking a series of questions to lead the witness down a certain route so that they end up contradicting themselves. They appear unreliable because their answer to the question changes when they are asked it again.

Weighing scales or kitchen scales are measurement tools which we depend on for reliability. When we weigh ourselves one day, we expect the scales to give the same reading if we step off the scales and on to them again. Hence they are reliable. With kitchen scales, we expect half a kilo of butter to weigh the same as half a kilo of flour, because it is the 'half a kilo' that is the reliable measurement. The fact that it is butter one time and flour the next does not matter.

THE VALIDITY AND RELIABILITY OF MARKING

The more objective a measurement is, the more likely it is to be valid and reliable. Over the course of your degree course you will write many essays and exam questions. These are then marked by lecturers. The mark you are awarded is based on their judgement against a set of marking criteria. The criteria are there to help maintain a level of objectivity, but essentially marking is a rather subjective activity. In order to improve the validity and reliability of marking a sample of marked essays are 'moderated', which means that a colleague also marks them and then discusses the mark with the original marker. If there is a lot of disagreement a third colleague becomes involved in the moderation process until agreement can be reached. After moderation, another sample is sent to an 'external examiner' who is an academic at another university, and they also mark the sample of work, checking that the marks given are in line with the standards and marks awarded at their institution. This process means that at least three different people with different opinions are looking at the work submitted, which increases the validity because the mark is then a representation of the essay submitted and not, for example, the lecturer's opinion of the student; it also increases the reliability because three people will have agreed the same marking standard for the same cohort of work.

SEARCHING THE LITERATURE

The concept of 'literature' at school is something that is studied in English. We read 'literature' which is generally fiction, often written some time ago. Most English Literature curriculums include Shakespeare, Charles Dickens, and other renowned authors of novels, plays or poetry.

In academia, literature has a different meaning. 'Literature' refers to all the previous academic studies that have been written in a field, such that a 'review of the literature' is not a book review in the sense of a summary of a particular book, but rather an overview of what different authors in the field being studied have said about that particular subject or issue.

Academic literature is also non-fiction – that is, it is not made up. Academic literature is the reporting of research studies that have been carried out and reviewed by peers in the field as being of a good enough standard to be worthy of publication.

SYSTEMATIC LITERATURE REVIEWS

A literature review therefore is a summary of what has been written in the field. The next question is how do you find out what has been written in the field? Basically you search through various electronic databases held in your institution's learning resource centre to find articles that are relevant and then you download those specific articles and read them.

Once you have found some good articles, a way of expanding your reading is to pick articles off the reference lists of those you have read and found useful. This is a very useful way of finding relevant reading. However, it is a little bit happenchance and you may come across things that are relevant or you may not.

A systematic literature review is one where you select your search terms and databases and then work through every item that is listed to assess its relevance. If you then happen to come across an article that is relevant but not generated by your search terms, you should ignore it as it hasn't been identified through your 'system'.

Be careful about calling a literature review systematic as it implies that you have had a system of searching and that you've adhered to it 100 per cent. Most people, therefore, just refer to their literature review and don't use the term 'systematic' at all.

A POTTED HISTORY OF UNIVERSITIES IN THE UK

Around the twelfth century, the noun *universitas* was used to describe a privileged corporate body. The original university in England was Oxford, and then in 1209 some of the Oxford masters broke away and established Cambridge. The split occurred over an argument around scientific nature, with Cambridge being renowned now for the sciences, and Oxford better known for the arts. There were also three universities in Scotland at that time: Glasgow, Edinburgh and St Andrews and this was the situation for a number of centuries – three in Scotland and two in England. It was only around the start of the sixteenth century that *universitas* narrowed its meaning to be a privileged corporate body of an academic community specialising in higher education. The first half of the nineteenth century saw the expansion of the sector with the ancient universities including Durham and the University of London, and two more in Aberdeen, Scotland.

In 1963 the Robbins Report was published which underpinned the foundations of the redbrick universities including Manchester, Leeds and Nottingham to name a few, as well as the creation of the polytechnic sector. Between 1965 and 1991 the polytechnics grew fivefold in student numbers and in the White Paper of 1991 the government announced that it was going to give the polytechnics degree-awarding powers and university status, unifying the sector. This happened in 1992. This was followed in 1997 by the Dearing Report, which was a government enquiry into the future of higher education, and universities now were no longer a privilege of the upper classes but a contributor to democracy and the economy with a utilitarian output.

Hence while universities were founded in the liberal traditions of education for the sake of education, they are now viewed from a more utilitarian perspective of education for the purpose of meaningful work, whatever that meaningful work might be.

Applying the purpose of higher education to your own motivation for coming to university

There are a number of views expressed in the literature as to the purpose of higher education. Seven are listed in the table opposite. Think about how these apply to you, and allocate a percentage to them so that you've allocated 100 per cent between them all as they apply to you. References are given as to whose work you might want to read to find out more about each view.

View	Percentage
The Educated Man – higher education is about the development of the educated person as a whole. The object is intellectual and the extension of knowledge rather than the advancement of knowledge (Newman, 1853)	
The Moral Society – the university promotes self-awareness, psychological well-being and human understanding such that it allows students to develop values and morals (Allen, 1988)	
The Promotion of Society (national prosperity) – the national agenda impacts on universities such that universities make the kind of people that society needs to sustain itself (Herbst, 1973)	
The Pursuit of Knowledge (research) – universities should create new knowledge that may or may not be used by industry, but is worthy as knowledge generation in its own right (Gibbons *et al.*, 1994)	
The Promotion of Democracy – the development of conflicting ideas and the concept of academic freedom promote democracy and choice and challenge the political ideas dominant at the time (Barnett, 1990)	
The Community (regional focus) – communities have a common bond and the university is both a learning community and a common bond within its local community and region (Christopherson, 1973)	
The Professional School (vocational) – the role of the university cannot be separated from the development of the individual for work (Jaspers, 1960)	

YOUR REASON FOR COMING TO UNIVERSITY

Other reasons for coming to university

Can you identify why you think you have come to university and what you hope to gain from the experience? Write yourself a list below of the specific reasons why you have chosen to come to university. Try to link each to one of the theories above:

Reason for coming to university	Link to theory

15

You should now have some idea of why you have come to university, and this may be very different to the theories offered on what universities are about. You may have come to have a good time, meet new people, and sit a few exams – and hopefully these reasons will also be fulfilled. However, that is not the purpose of your being at university. The purpose of you coming to university is to develop you as a critical, disciplined and independent thinker; an intellectual who can sustain an argument and a person that is highly employable when you leave.

DISCIPLINED THINKING

It is interesting also to note down now what you think you will take away as your quality measures when you finish your studies. Make a list of the things you will take into account when recommending your course/university to others when you finish.

Quality measures
1
2
3
4
5
6

I suspect, although I could be wrong, that your list of quality measures is not that similar to your list of reasons for coming to university. This is the first lesson in disciplined thinking. Many students include in their reasons for coming to university something like 'to get a good job', or 'to get a good degree'. However, their quality measures are not 'the job I get at the end of my degree', or 'the classification of the degree', but rather include such factors as 'the quality of the lecturers', 'the social life', and so forth. It is important that you measure outcomes by what you are trying to achieve. If you came to university to listen to great lectures, then by all means use the quality of the lecturers as your measure – but they are not a good measure against coming to university in order to get a good job.

CHAPTER SUMMARY

This chapter has hopefully given you an insight into the academic world of the university, some of the language that has developed within the context and why it may have developed that way over time. You may find you have come to university for career prospects and a better future, which is the utilitarian philosophy, but your university is holding on to the traditions of liberalism, and hence your experience may be a peculiar mix of traditions combined with your more modern requirements. This book hopes to guide you through the traditions by teaching you the techniques you need to know in order to perform best in this environment.

BUSINESS GAME

Each chapter will end with the learning from the chapter being applied to a business scenario so that you can see how the learning process at university is also relevant in 'real life'.

A large company that makes and sells oven-ready frozen meals is experiencing some difficulties. It cannot cope with the amount of business it is receiving. It needs to expand but does not have enough people with the right skills and knowledge to be able to do so. A consultancy firm is called for advice and the consultants recommend that the company recruits some local graduates to help it out.

Give five reasons why the consultants would recommend local graduates:

1 _____

2 _____

3 _____

4 _____

5 _____

There could be lots of reasons for the choice of graduates. Hopefully your answers might have included something like:

- Graduates are skilled critical thinkers and therefore take a disciplined approach to problem solving.

- Graduates have a pool of knowledge and skills that they have learnt throughout their studies that they can apply to the business' problems.

- Graduates have developed skills in learning, and they should continue learning, ensuring that mistakes don't happen twice.

- Graduates have developed a sense of enquiry that leads them to ask questions and search for the truth, which is useful in problem solving.

- Local graduates will have knowledge of the local environment having lived in it, and will be able to use this knowledge in problem solving.

References

Allen, M. (1988) *The Goals of Universities.* Buckingham: SRHE and Open University Press.

Barnett, R. (1990) *The Idea of Higher Education.* Buckingham: SRHE and Open University Press.

Christopherson, D. (1973) *The University at Work.* London: SCM Press Ltd.

Dearing, Sir Ron (1997) Report of the National Committee of Inquiry into Higher Education. Available via http://www.elearning.ac.uk/resources/clearing.

Gibbon, M., Limoges, C., Nowotny, H., Schwartzman, S., Scott, P. & Trow, M. (1994) *The New Production of Knowledge: The dynamics of science and research in contemporary societies.* London: Sage Publications Ltd.

Herbst, P. (1973) Work, Labour and University Education. In Peters, R. S. (Ed) *The Philosophy of Education.* Oxford: Oxford University Press, Ch.2.

Jaspers, K. (1960) *The Idea of the University.* London: Peter Owen.

Newman, H. (1853) *The Idea of a University.* Reprinted in London: Yale University Press.

(Robbins, Chairman) Committee on Higher Education (1963) *Higher Education Report of the Committee appointed by the Prime Minister under the Chairmanship of Lord Robbins 1961–1963.* London: HMSO.

2 ▶ HOW TO READ AN ACADEMIC ARTICLE AND MAKE NOTES

This chapter focuses on your reading skills so that you can become a more efficient and effective reader while at university. You will learn how to read for a specific purpose and make notes on your reading, so that you never need to read the same thing twice. Referencing is also covered in this chapter in great depth. Plagiarism is the academic offence of copying so it is absolutely vital that you learn how to reference properly so that you do not accidently commit plagiarism.

This chapter will cover:

- Choosing what to read for different purposes
- Making notes from reading
- Referencing

USING THIS CHAPTER

INTRODUCTION

This chapter basically helps you with reading. Reading is an absolutely key skill in academic life and there are ways of doing it that are efficient, effective, quick and economical, and then there are the ways that most other students do it. Much of this chapter is taught to doctoral students at the start of their research – when they have already completed their undergraduate and masters degrees – and they get really cross with themselves for not having engaged in this manner of reading earlier, because essentially all the reading they've done previously needs to be reread. While everyone at university can 'read' per se, when you read for academic purposes you are not reading simply to get through a text, you are reading so that you can use that text to support your thinking or line of argument, and to some extent to prove that you are aware that that piece of research has been done and you know that it is there. There are some real tricks to the art of reading and this chapter helps you get to grips with these.

WHY READ?

It may sound like a silly question to ask, but why do we read when we study? How does reading help us? Basically we read to find out what other people have found out before us. This prevents us from reinventing the wheel.

We read to find out more about a subject; what other people think about something; what other people have found out about something; or how other people explain something.

Think about some of the things you read everyday without thinking about why you read them. Try to note down why you actually read them.

What you read	Why do you read it?
Newspaper	
Map	
Menu	
Recipe	
Post	
E-mail	
Others	

You might read the newspaper to find out what is happening in the world; you read a map to find the best way to get to where you want to go; you read a menu so that you can make a decision about what to eat; you read a recipe so that you know how to make something; you read your post to see what someone has sent you, i.e. what it is that someone else wants you to know; and you read your e-mail for the same reason. Basically you read to gain information – either to help you make a decision, or because someone has sent you the information, or because it is information that you want to know for a particular reason.

WHAT TO READ

There are three main sources that you can read from: books, journals, and the internet.

Books can take the form of authored books (textbooks) or edited books. If a book is authored, as this one is, then one person (or two or three as named on the front cover) has written the whole book and the book is usually a textbook. If a book is edited, then different people have written each chapter and the editors (named on the front cover) have put the collection of chapters together and written the linkages between them as well as the introduction. Edited books are more like journal articles as each chapter is written by a specialist in that specific area, usually reporting on some research that they have carried out. Textbooks therefore help you to under-stand a subject by giving explanations, exercises to work through, key learning points, and other aids to help you learn about a subject. Edited books present dif-ferent authors' views on specific subject areas, usually around their research.

Journals are generally peer-reviewed, which means that other academics have read the article and approved of what it says. This is a form of quality assurance, and some journals are recognised as being of better quality than others. There are various journal rankings that can tell you which ones are the best in the field, but you don't need to get too hung up on that at this stage. Most of your course hand-books will give you a recommended list of journals to consult so that should be your starting point.

Journal articles generally report on a piece of research carried out in the field of the author's choice. The research is written up in a particular format and submitted to a journal for publication, at which point other academics read it and review it and, if it is deemed to be a good enough piece of research, it is published. Academics are not paid to write journal articles; they do it because it is part of the academic game of raising your research profile and standing in the field. An academic's publishing record is one of the factors that helps them gain their title and status of 'Professor'.

Textbooks do not count for much in the academic recognition game among aca-demics, but they are recognised by students, and the authors do get paid for writing them – usually in the form of a royalty. With edited books, the editors get a royalty fee and the chapter writers don't get any money, but these chapters do carry some weight in academic circles and count towards promotions. This information should make no difference to you at all, it is simply here so that you understand the differences between the two forms. Textbooks are of a different nature because you are paid to write them and they are a support for teaching and learning. Edited books and journal articles are written because the academic wants to put their research and/or opinion into the public domain for debate and consideration. Journal articles in particular are not written with students in mind, and hence they can sometimes be quite difficult to read.

The internet is a great source of data as you can type in virtually any search term and come up with pages and pages of information to read. The problem with the internet is much of it is not peer-reviewed so there is no quality mechanism to check that what people are putting on the web is any way accurate. There is a specific academic search engine called 'google scholar' which can be accessed from https://scholar.google.co.uk and searches for academic sources only, but even this links to university web pages and Wikipedia, none of which have been quality assured for accuracy. Also, pages on the internet can change whenever the author wishes to change them, so when you reference an internet page, make sure you always note down the date on which you accessed it.

THE IMPORTANCE OF REFERENCING

It is absolutely vital to your survival at university that you learn how to reference, and that you do so from day 1. When you reference someone you are acknowledging their work. Basically you are telling the reader that this idea/view was presented by this author, and if they want to find out more about it, they can look up the reference list or bibliography at the end of the article or book and get the full citation or listing.

If you do not reference then it looks like you are trying to pass someone else's idea off as your own. This is cheating in the academic world and you will disciplined for the academic offence of plagiarism. If you are found to be guilty of plagiarism you may find yourself kicked out of university without any qualification. This can be a particularly hard penalty if you are in your final year, but it has happened.

There are various ways in which you can reference work as a number of different systems have developed over the years and in different subject disciplines. It is better to get the referencing convention wrong than not to reference at all. If you use the wrong convention or form of referencing you may have a mark or two deducted, but you will not get kicked out of university. If you do not reference at all then you may get kicked out of university – particularly if you do it consistently.

HOW TO REFERENCE

There are various different referencing conventions but the most frequently used format is known as the 'Harvard Style of Referencing'. This involves citing the author and the year of publication in the text itself (with a page number if you are using a direct quote), and then having a list of references at the end of the essay which gives the reader the full details of the source. It's probably easiest to demonstrate this by showing some examples. Below is a passage of text, and then the relevant bits of the reference list are given after the passage. The excerpt demonstrates the referencing of a textbook, an edited chapter in a book, a journal article and a website so that you can see how each is represented. See if you can identify which is which.

A demographic shift is changing the nature of the employment contract, such that workers are more able to pick and choose between employers based on issues such as work life balance, diversity policy, and the extent to which they will have a voice (Berger, 2004). The employee is less a malleable resource for the company and more a mobile investor of his or her own intellectual, social and emotional capitals, and as such are 'volunteer' employees for organisations, who view themselves not as assets, but as investors in their organisations (Gratton & Ghoshal, 2003). Boole (2004) even recommends that organisations use outplacement techniques to sharpen the mutual understanding of an employee's current and future potential contribution to the organisation, so that there are no misunderstandings in the career transition processes, or in what they are volunteering to. The labour market of the future will favour the employee, and this has rebalanced and is hence redefining the nature of the psychological contract (Beardwell & Holden, 2001).

A Towers Perrin study 'How leading organisations manage talent' examined 22 large employers and found that talent management is now a strategic business priority. In industries such as PR, where intellectual property is everything and accounts move when people do, finding a way to keep the best talent is everything (Towers Perrin, 2002). While the instinct might be to find out what other companies are doing and copycat their practices, they may not be the right practice for your company. Boole suggests recognising the key employees on which your business depends and attempting to understand how to better meet their needs. Lex Werner of The Limited found that the company's results improved dramatically when he spent half his time on people rather than half his time on finances (Handfield-Jones, Michaels & Axelrod, 2001). It would appear that if you manage the right people in the right way, the finances look after themselves.

References:

Bannister, L. 2005. Tips on Talent Management. *Campaign*, 32–33.

Beardwell, I. & Holden, L. 2001. *Human Resource Management: A contemporary approach.* Harlow: Prentice Hall.

Berger, D. R. 2004. The journey to organisation excellence: navigating the forces impacting talent management. In D. R. Berger & L. A. Berger (Eds.), *The Talent Management Handbook.* Ch.3. New York: McGraw-Hill.

Boole, G. 2004. Using outplacement techniques to evaluate employees. In D. R. Berger & L. A. Berger (Eds.), *The Talent Management Handbook.* Ch.14. New York: McGraw-Hill.

Branham, L. 2005. Planning to Become an Employer of Choice. *Journal of Organizational Excellence,* 24(3), 57–68.

Gratton, L. & Ghoshal, S. 2003. Managing Personal Human Capital: New Ethos for the 'Volunteer' Employee. *European Management Journal,* 21(1), 1–10.

Handfield-Jones, H., Michaels, E. & Axelrod, B. 2001. Talent Management: A critical part of every leader's job. *Ivey Business Journal,* 66(2), 53–59.

Towers Perrin. 2002. *How Leading Organisations Manage Talent.* @ www.towersperrin.com/tp/getwebcachedoc?webc=HRS/USA/2002/200210/TM_Best_ Practices.pdf. Accessed November 2004.

Source: Taken from Blass, E. (Ed) (2008). *Talent Management: Cases and Commentary.* London: Palgrave.

Note how you cannot tell the difference between the types of source within the text, but only in the reference list at the end. This is because the Harvard system of referencing is an author:date system whereby you cite the author's surname and the date of publication (year only) in the text itself, and then the full details of the source in the reference list. If you don't know part of the reference, then say 'unknown'. Admitting that it is not your own idea but you don't know where they came from is better than trying to pass them off as your own. Even though you have reworded what someone has said, they still had the idea first.

In the example passage above, we don't know who wrote the Towers Perrin report, hence we simply accredit it to Towers Perrin. Equally, if you quote someone directly, i.e. copy exactly what they said because you don't want to reword it for whatever reason, then you have to cite the page number also. This would lead to a reference appearing in the text in the following format:

> Blass (2008:16) claims 'intellectual property has an added value and talented workers take their intellectual property with them when they move'.

The important point is that you appreciate that you *must* reference your work or you will be investigated for plagiarism. The internet has made it much easier for academics to catch people plagiarising work. We only need to type part of a sentence into google and the internet often finds us the source. There are also specific search packages for academics looking to check out plagiarism. It is obvious to us when we read a piece of work when something has been plagiarised as it is of a different style to the rest of the work.

Referencing secondary sources

Primary sources are the original sources that are quoted. Secondary sources are the primary sources referred to by other authors – such as in textbooks. Wherever possible go back and source the primary material, but otherwise cite the secondary source in the text as having referred to the primary source. So for example you might find something like this:

> The Old Bakery was knocked down in 1786 (Brown, 1790, in Hardwell, 2006).

The reference in the references list would then be:

Hardwell, J. (2006) *The History of Lockwood.* London: Palgrave.

Referencing books

In the text you state the author and the year, and the page number if it is a direct quote. If there are more than two authors, then use the abbreviation '*et al.*' after the first author to denote 'and others'. Hence a sentence might look like:

Brown (1790) records the Old Bakery as being knocked down in 1786. This may be inaccurate as Heron and Birch (1788) refer to the Old Bakery as being in situ in their analysis of letters from residents of Lockwood, while the Lockwood Parishioners record the 'demise of the Bakery' in the early 1800's (Monty *et al.*, 1820: 23).

The reference list would then look like this:

Brown, F (1790) *Lockwood Diaries.* Lockwood: Century Press.

Heron, G. & Birch, K. (1788) Letters from Lockwood in Brookwell, S. (Ed) *A History of Lockwood.* Lockwood: Century Press.

Monty, D., Slater, R., Moss, H. & Jasper, L. (1820) *Memoirs from Parishioners of Lockwood.* Lockwood: Century Press.

Referencing journal articles

The citation in the text will look exactly the same as for books, but the reference list will give the article title and the journal title in the following format:

Hardwell, J. (2007) A reflection on the historical recordings of Lockwood. *Journal of English History and Heritage.* 39(2), pp27–46.

Note the 39(2), pp27–46 means volume 39, issue 2, pages 27–46.

Referencing the internet

Again, if you know the author of the web page, the citation in the text will remain as author and year. If you don't know the author of the web page, use the 'anon' abbreviation of 'anonymous' to denote the author and then note the year. If you have more than one anonymous citation then you need to note the first one as 'anon (2008a)' and then the next will be 'anon (2008b)' and so forth.

In terms of the reference list, the format should be:

Anonymous (2008a) Reflections on Lockwood. Available at http://www.lockwood.co.uk/memoirs.htm [Accessed: 20 August 2008].

WHAT EXACTLY IS PLAGIARISM?

Some students get themselves into a panic over whether something has been pla-giarised or not. After all, you are encouraged to read and work with other people's ideas, so it seems strange to then get punished for discussing them. The point is not that you are discussing and using someone else's idea, but how you refer to those other people's ideas. If you try to pass them off as your own ideas and words then that is plagiarism. If you say that the idea came from someone else and you then name them and the idea, then that is fine.

If you copy someone else's words, put quote marks around them and reference them correctly then that is fine. If you copy someone else's work and don't do this but allow the reader to think that these are your words, then that is plagiarism.

It is possible that you can get yourself to a point where you've read so much that you can't say where the idea came from but you know it stems from your reading. In such a case, you can say something like the following:

> Many authors have discussed the issues of leadership and management (see, for example, Ghoshal, 2004; Adair, 2005; Grint, 2007; and Peters, 2006) debating whether the two are the same or differ.

You would then put all four of these references in your reference list at the end of your submission.

The important thing to ask yourself is 'have I told the reader where this has come from?' If the answer is Yes, then you will not be guilty of plagiarism; if the answer is No, then you are likely to find yourself in trouble. There is very sophisticated soft-ware now for tracking plagiarism so very few students get away with it. Also, it defies the point of undertaking your studies and doesn't benefit you in the long run.

If you find yourself in a complete panic because you have not done an assignment and have to hand something in the next day do not copy something. You are better to hand in nothing and record a fail grade and resubmit than you are to hand in something copied. If you get done for plagiarism, the penalty is much worse than failing and resubmitting.

So, basic message with regard to plagiarism – don't do it!

HOW TO MAKE NOTES AND KEEP A RECORD OF YOUR READING

There are various ways in which people make notes when they are reading. Some people write on their textbook or journal article, highlighting phrases in the text, or underlining them, or writing comments in the margins. While this may work for them at the time, it is not a productive means of note-taking for the future. You cannot go back and see what you gained from the reading without basically reading it again. Hence it is important to note down the passages you have underlined or highlighted (with the page numbers so you know they are direct quotes), and the notes that you have written for yourself in the margin, on another sheet of paper or in a database.

The most effective and efficient means of note-taking is to use some form of database. Some people find they have to do this on paper, which is fine, but still not as efficient as doing it electronically. The main reason for taking notes in a database format is that you can then use them again and again throughout your studies. You will be amazed at how often you can use the same sources to make different points and different lines of argument. If you keep your notes in a database then you can search the database for notes you've made relating to different topics or search terms. This allows the database to remind you of everything you have already read that might be relevant, which gives you a head start on your reading rather than feeling you know nothing about a topic.

EndNote is a fantastic software package for keeping notes of your reading as it allows you to search your notes by key words or words appearing in your notes or abstracts, or however you want to search. There may be other equally suitable packages for the job, indeed any database package should suffice, but EndNote has been specifically designed for referencing and compiling bibliographies, and indeed it can link through to your word processing package and create your reference list or bibliography for you as you reference throughout the text. Enough said about EndNote – this is not a lesson on how to use it; you can get the manual with package to work it out. This is a chapter about how to read and make notes.

There are three important elements to note-taking: the reference information for your reference list and bibliography; your key points and quotes from the text; and the author's key points and quotes from the text. Now you're probably asking yourself why would your key points and quotes be different to the author's key points and quotes? Good question. When an author writes something they do so for a purpose. They want to present a particular line of argument. When you read something, you are also doing so for a purpose. That purpose is unlikely to be the same as the author's, and hence you may find different points of what they write more important than the argument they are trying to make.

Overleaf is an example of an abstract written by the authors, and the summary notes written by a student, and the referencing details. Note how the first two elements differ. Can you see what the authors' and student's agendas are?

Abstract: Two paradigm shifts are discussed here: talentship and sustainability. First, the traditional service-oriented HR focus must be extended to a 'decision science' that enhances decisions about human capital. We call this decision science talentship. It includes talent segmentation, or identifying pivotal talent pools where the quality and/or availability of human capital makes the biggest difference to strategic success. Second, HR and business leaders increasingly define organisational effectiveness beyond traditional financial outcomes to encompass sustainability – achieving success today without compromising the needs of the future. A common strategic human capital decision science can reveal pivotal talent under both traditional and sustainability based definitions, and thus uncover important insights about the talent implications of the shifting definition of strategic success.

Summary: What are the talent pools (jobs, roles or competencies) that a 20% improvement in quality or availability would make the biggest difference to organisational success? These should be the targets for HR investment and leader attention. Talent segmentation is as vital as customer segmentation. Definition of organisational success is shifting from financial returns to sustainability. Need to look at impact, effectiveness and efficiency in decision science to look beyond financial returns at wider sustainability issues. This then leads to talent application in different areas that would previously not be considered.

Reference: Boudreau, J. W. & Ramstad, P. M. 2005. Talentship, Talent Segmentation, and Sustainability: A new HR decision science paradigm for a new strategy definition. *Human Resource Management*, 44(2), 129–136.

The two differ because the authors are trying to establish the case for the concept of 'talentship' and hence their aim with the article is to study the decision science within HRM which occurs when human capital theory is applied to talent management. The student, on the other hand, is interested in how organisations are defining their talent pools as part of the talent management process, and hence has drawn from the article a very different set of notes to that which the authors would propose. This is fine – everyone reads different things into what someone is saying, but that is why it is good to record the authors' abstract/summary as well as this gives you a record of what they think their work is about.

How to read an academic article

Academic articles generally take a similar form regardless of the journal in which they are published. If an article varies significantly from this form, then it is a pretty good indication that the journal is not a peer-reviewed academic journal but more of an industry or trade journal. Academic articles usually have the following elements:

1 *Abstract* – this is a summary of what the author thinks the paper is about. Copy this into your database as it is good to keep a record.

2 *Introduction* – this can be a useful overview of the state of play in the area prior to this article being written, and tells you why the authors chose to look into this particular issue.

3 *Some form of literature review* – sometimes this is included in the introduction. This is useful if you are doing an in-depth study and want to know what else you should be looking at as it is an overview of the relevant literature in the field. However, often it is more detail than you need to know for your particular purposes, and hence you can skip over this section on your first read.

4 *Methodology* – this is where the authors describe what they have actually done in their piece of research, how they went about it, and how they analysed the results. This is the bit that the peer-reviewers will have scrutinised to check that it is valid and reliable (see Chapter 1). Unless you are thinking of replicating a study, you are unlikely to need to understand in any great depth the methodology that has been employed. You may be interested to know if they used interviews, or a questionnaire, or some other methodology but the detail is not going to be important to you at this stage in your studies, and will probably not make much sense to you. Hence, skip over this section.

5 *Results* – this is where the authors present their findings. Sometimes this is quite interesting, other times it is confusing, particularly if it is table after table of complicated statistics. At first read, you can skip over this section.

6 *Discussion* – this is the important section. This is where the authors discuss what they have found out in relation to what was known before (i.e. the literature) and what it means in practice. This is the section that is most important for you to read.

7 *Conclusions* – this is the authors' attempt to conclude from their study what they found out and where this leaves us all. Academics are not always the best at writing conclusions and this section tends to be weaker than the discussion. However, it is quite short and should probably be read on first viewing.

So, the first time you read the article, note the referencing details in your database, copy out the abstract, and then read the introduction and discussion making notes of key quotes (with page numbers) or issues that you might want to use again. Having read these sections you should be able to say in two or three sentences what the article is telling you. Write these notes down in your database also.

Now you need to make a decision – is the article so important to what you are looking at that you want to read more of it or not? If not, put it aside and save the database entry. If yes, read the results and literature review also. Make further notes in your database entry.

There are two other points about articles that are worth noting: diagrams and the reference list.

If there is a really good diagram/model, this may give you an overview of the whole paper in one page. If this is the case, copy the model/diagram and either attach it electronically to your database, or make a note of the fact that you have the model in your database and keep a hard copy somewhere safe. Good diagrams/models are a gift in an article as they should basically tell you everything that the article is about in one view, saving you a lot of time and effort in reading.

The reference list is also important. Sometimes it can be difficult to know what to read because your search term can produce thousands of results and there is too much there to consider, or your search term reveals very little. If this happens, a good journal article can provide you with lots of other sources to read. Skim down the reference list and have a look at what the author of the article read and referred to – some of their reading might also be relevant to you and you can look out those sources and read them also.

How to read a textbook

A textbook has been written as a teaching and learning aid with the student in mind. It is likely to be a summary of lots of other writers in the field, giving explanations of key theories and ideas, and exercises to help you apply the learning to your studies. While you can dip in and out of a textbook, each chapter is designed to be worked through from start to finish, and the chapters usually follow a logical order such that each chapter builds on the previous one. Hence they are really designed for you to read from start to finish.

Course textbooks rarely tell you something new. They are a collective summary of the field you are studying and hence generally tell you about other authors' ideas. They are good because they allow you to see lots of different authors' ideas next to each other, and give you a good overview of the whole field you are looking at. They do not, however, go into any detail about how an author got to their view, nor do they generally evaluate those views. They simply offer an overview of the field to help you generally understand the subject area you are studying.

In terms of making notes from textbooks, you want to note down the key theories that are referred to, and work through the learning exercises as they have genuinely been designed to help your thought and learning processes, and not simply to fill the page.

Textbooks are the most difficult to keep notes on in EndNote or your chosen database package as there is likely to be quite a lot of material. You could start a new entry for each chapter in the textbook, but that isn't really the purpose of textbooks. You read textbooks in order to gain understanding and a general baseline of knowledge. You don't really read textbooks to develop a line of argument or make a case for or against something, because that isn't really what they are for.

So, in terms of note-taking from a textbook, make sure you have all the key theories that the authors are referring to – if you're really clever you can make separate database entries for each one and reference the original source that the textbook authors reference, and then go back and look at these original sources at a future point to embellish what you've got from the textbook. If you copy from the textbook into your database make sure that you reference the textbook and which page you have copied from so that you are not plagiarising.

How to read an edited book and take notes

Edited books have chapters written by different authors, and 'linkage' elements written by the editor, either in the form of an introduction and conclusion only, or section introductions as you proceed through the book. It is worth having a quick read over the introduction as it will guide you as to which bits of the book interest you and which chapters you want to read fully. You are unlikely to want to make notes from the introduction unless there is a particular quote that you like and might want to use again.

Once you've decided which chapters to read, make notes from those chapters in your database as you would an article. Hence you need to record all the reference detail first, which includes the authors and title of the chapter and the editors and title of the book. Then write yourself a summary of each subsection of the chapter (there are usually subheadings) so that you put into one or two sentences what that subsection is telling you. Remember to note down the page numbers of any direct quotes that you include.

What to record and not record in the database

EndNote alters the screen information to complete according to what type of source you are recording. This is helpful as it prompts you to make sure you've got the right information for recording the references of that particular source. EndNote also gives you the option of recording information that you don't need. An example of a completed EndNote record is overleaf. This records everything you need for the reference, plus keywords the database owner has allocated to a record, plus the authors' abstract and their own notes. Note though, if you look at EndNote, how many of the fields are left blank as they are superfluous to our needs.

EndNote also has the facility to read referencing details from academic databases but this is quite a complicated process and beyond the scope of this chapter. This chapter is not about how to use EndNote as a package per se, but more about how you can personally use EndNote as a reading database. EndNote will also create your bibliography for you if you link it through to Word, for example, but again you would need to consult the EndNote manual on how to do this – for the purposes of this chapter you just need to know that it can be done.

Reference Type: Book Section

Record Number: 42

Author: Burnett, T.; Kettleborough, S.

Year: 2006

Title: New Frontiers for Diversity and Inclusion

Editor: April, K.; Shockley, M.

Book Title: Diversity: New realities in a changing world.

City: Hampshire

Publisher: Palgrave

Pages: 102–110

Short Title: New Frontiers for Diversity and Inclusion

Keywords: Diversity; Inclusion

Notes: Diversity is often a game of percentages, where the rules state that the organisations must frantically hire visibly different people in order to hit targets or quotas. Inclusion is about creating environments where all people can prosper and progress irrespective of race, colour, gender, physical ability, age, religion, sexual orientation or belief. Identify a number of myths in business and society:

1. Global governance supports a level playing field. Wealth is not equally distributed.
2. It's about race . . . and it's black and white. The white man has always ruled so they can't see what the problem is.
3. The best person should get the job. Definition of 'best person' is usually biased.
4. Inclusion is a moral issue, not a commercial issue. The business case varies for every organisation.
5. Inclusion boils down to good HR management and some training. Need to get leadership buy-in, grow your own culture, have inclusive values, and get the dialogue right.

Example of the fields you need to complete in EndNote

WHERE TO FIND 'THE LITERATURE'

You may think that you will find the literature in 'the library' but that is not always the case. Most universities and colleges no longer have 'libraries' as such, but rather learning resource centres (LRC) or learning information centres (LIC). Much of the material that was previously held as paper copy in a library is now held electronically and can be accessed anywhere, anytime, from any computer. The LRC is always a good place to go though, as there are usually computer terminals for you to use, and it is still the home of books that are not electronic books, and back-copies of journals that have not yet been digitalised. Most are usually staffed by experts who can help you find what you are looking for if you get stuck. If your institution offers a tour or induction to the LRC, do it! It is not a walk around a library and it will save you lots of time later on in your studies and stop you from having to ask stupid questions of support staff.

Your LRC is likely to have a catalogue of the books that it holds that you can search through in the LRC itself. Some institutions let you search this remotely and reserve items so that you can then go in and pick them up.

Most journals are now accessed electronically and your institution will have sub-scribed to many journals, but probably not all the journals available in the whole world. Hence you may still have to make the odd request for a copy of a journal article through the 'inter-library loan' service which your LRC staff will be able to help you with.

The easiest way to search for relevant journal articles is to use one of the many subject databases that exist, such as ProQuest or Ebsco in Business; ERIC in Education; Lawtel in Law and so forth. These databases allow you to enter a search term and then they list all of the articles that they find that meet your search criteria. There is a real art to searching for relevant literature. Usually, initial searches result in thousands of hits so you need to be clever about the words you use for searching.

For example, the excerpt used earlier in this chapter is about 'talent management' as used in the business and management context. A search for 'talent management' revealed very few articles as it is a relatively new concept in the field. A search for 'management' was endless, and a search for 'talent' brought up articles about artists and dancers that weren't relevant to the work being carried out. Hence search terms were used which were allied to the field, such as 'succession planning' as this was an activity that talent management has subsumed, or 'selection' com-bined with 'high potentials', and other ideas such as this.

USING YOUR DATABASE FOR LITERATURE REVIEWS

If you become disciplined from day one and record everything that you read in your electronic database then you will be amazed at how quickly you build up your records and it won't be long before you've read over 100 articles. As you move from module to module in your course, you will study subject areas that build on the pre-vious modules, and hence much of your reading will still be relevant. When you get a new assignment to write, the first thing you should do is key your search terms into your own database of your notes from reading. This should reveal a number of articles that are relevant to your new topic area that you would not have thought of had you not recorded them electronically and gives you an instant start to your next assignment as you may have 10 references already. This allows you to use your reading as widely as possible, most efficiently, and most effectively.

FINDING THE TIME TO READ

Think about how you spend your day and where you have dead time – that is time when you are not actually achieving anything. This could be travelling time, waiting time, or an hour in between lectures when you have nothing timetabled.

You should always carry an article with you that you need to read. You'll be amazed at how you can read an article in half an hour if you follow the guidelines above, but if you can't immediately record it into your database, make notes in the margin and then spend 10 minutes typing it in at the end of the day. You'll find that you read lots if you do this, and you won't feel like you're wasting time when you have dead time.

CHAPTER SUMMARY

This chapter has taught you how to read effectively and efficiently. You do not need to read every word within an article, chapter or book; you only need to read those elements that are going to inform your thinking or argument. The most important thing about reading is to record your notes in a manner which allows them to be used on more than one occasion. The best way to do this is through an electronic database such as EndNote. Searching through your database of reading enables you to use articles you have read for one assignment over and over again.

BUSINESS GAME

You have gone to work for the frozen food company as a young graduate. The company wants you to spend three months researching the market for their products in Brazil. How would you go about this?

There are many ways this could be tackled. Going to your local university library would be a good starting point as they are likely to hold MINTEL and other marketing reports which will tell you about the Brazilian market in general. You need to gain access to a good academic database and a good marketing database and

Month 1:
Month 2:
Month 3:

enter the search terms 'Brazil food' and 'Brazil frozen food' and see what you come up with.

You might also, if you have time in month 3, review what the company has done in other overseas markets and see how directly transferable some of the ideas are to Brazil.

3 ▶ THE ART OF DISCIPLINE

This chapter helps you manage your time. Your timetable may seem relatively empty compared to school or college, but you are expected to do a lot of studying on your own. This requires self-discipline and good time management. By planning your time well, you will find that you have little time to waste and are always busy, rather than having a rush at assignment deadline time.

This chapter will cover:

- Planning your week to ensure you make good use of your time
- Combining different learning methods including lectures and seminars
- Planning workload for assessments

USING THIS CHAPTER

INTRODUCTION

Being successful at university is about self-discipline, and this is where it can differ from school. Students who progress to university from FE colleges often find the transition easier than those who come from sixth forms at schools, as they have already experienced the more independent approach to studying and less formalised management of the day that dominates the university experience. This chapter gives you some tips on how to manage your time at university in a manner that gives you the discipline to succeed with the flexibility to have fun. The key to succeeding at studies is good time management; and good time management is dependent on good stress management; and good stress management is dependent on a lot of other factors.

THE TYPICAL ACADEMIC WEEK

You may find that your timetable is populated with more 'free lessons' than lectures and seminars. Indeed, there may be some days when you don't even have to go into

Table 3.1

Time	Monday	Tuesday	Wednesday	Thursday	Friday
9–10					Lecture 3
10–11					Seminar 3
11–12	Lecture 1				
12–1		Seminar 2			
1–2					
2–3					
3–4	Seminar 1				Lecture 4
4–5	Seminar 4				
5–6		Lecture 2			

the university at all. This is because university study is based on the concept of the student being an independent learner, and hence the onus is on you the student to engage in your learning through whatever means you find most convenient and suitable for you. This might involve reading, it might involved writing, making notes, talking to peers, or using the internet or an e-learning facility. The point is, that is up to you to work out what helps you learn and engage in that activity. Note that talking to peers in this context means talking about your studies, not simply catching up on gossip over a coffee.

A typical timetable for an undergraduate student studying arts, humanities, social sciences or business is likely to look something like Table 3.1.

Evening lectures are becoming more common as they allow courses that have low entry numbers to run as evening courses as well, attracting additional part-time students on to the module.

There are a number of points to note here that could lead to bad habits and cause concern:

1 Two days a week there are no lessons timetabled, and hence no 'reason' for you to go into university.
2 There are long gaps between lectures and seminars on two occasions.
3 There is a lecture scheduled for 9am on a Friday morning, and Thursday night is usually 'the student night out'.

COMBINING WORKING AND STUDYING

For many students, this is a very good timetable as many of you will need to earn extra money while you are studying, and this timetable gives you the opportunity to work for two days a week during the week, as well as the possibility of working at weekends. Typical student employment is in local supermarkets or fast-food establishments where they can be more flexible about shift patterns and easily accommodate part-time workers.

Pub work or bar work is another way in which students can earn money, and is evening-based so shouldn't interfere with the day job of studying. This can also be a means of getting yourself out in the evening while earning money instead of spending it. Jobs within the student union bars are usually very popular and go quickly so it is worth approaching your student union for a job before you start if you are particularly keen to work for them.

If we fit working into the typical student timetable, it may start to look something like Table 3.2.

Table 3.2

Time	Monday	Tuesday	Wednesday	Thursday	Friday	Saturday	Sunday
9–10				Job at Tesco	Lecture 3	Job at Tesco	
10–11					Seminar 3		
11–12	Lecture 1						
12–1		Seminar 2					Bar job
1–2							
2–3							
3–4	Seminar 1				Lecture 4		
4–5	Seminar 4						
5–6		Lecture 2					
6–7	Bar job				Bar job		
7–8							
8–9							

This timetable is now starting to look quite busy. You have a 16-hour contract with Tesco, and two nights plus Sunday lunchtime at the local pub. Mondays are quiet nights so you cover the bar with only one other person. Sundays are packed with people wanting lunch. Friday nights are busy at the bar rather than with food so it feels much like socialising as well as working.

THE IMPORTANCE OF A DAY OFF

Wednesday is now looking like the only day you have 'off' all week. Given Wednesday afternoons are reserved as far as possible for sports at universities, this is a good day to have as your free day as you can engage in sports and social activity around the university campus.

It is important to have a day that you consider to be your day off so that you do have a day to relax, catch up, do the washing and shopping, and so forth without feeling guilty for taking time out from your studies.

If you try to study every day then you become burnt out with it, and bored, so it is important to give yourself a day off. Studying should be considered the same as any other job, and six days a week is enough.

It is also important to give yourself a couple of lie-ins when you have earned them, and some socialising time, much like everyone else. It is unlikely that you will get up early on a Sunday in the frame of mind for studying, so you might as well allocate it as a day to lie in, making it a legitimate thing to do. Knowing you have two days a week to sleep in can help you be disciplined about getting up on the other five days and getting going.

Once you start to put these on your timetable (Table 3.3), it starts to get quite full and you can see how little time you actually have left for studying – hence the need to be disciplined about it.

Table 3.3

Time	Monday	Tuesday	Wednesday	Thursday	Friday	Saturday	Sunday
9–10			Lie in	Job at Tesco	Lecture 3	Job at Tesco	Lie in
10–11					Seminar 3		
11–12	Lecture 1		Shopping				
12–1		Seminar 2	Washing				Bar job
1–2			Lazy lunch				
2–3			Sports				
3–4	Seminar 1				Lecture 4		
4–5	Seminar 4						
5–6		Lecture 2	Evening off socialising				
6–7	Bar job				Bar job		
7–8						Evening off socialising	
8–9							

FITTING IN THE STUDYING

Now that you start to look at your week there isn't actually that much time for studying. This is why you need to be disciplined about it. Chapter 2 guided you on how to read. As you become more skilled and practised at reading you will find that you can get through most academic articles in less than an hour. The same is true for a chapter of an edited book. A textbook might take a bit longer, but remember that you don't have to read every page and every chapter – only those that are relevant to what you are studying.

Ideally, you want to try to read something every day as you'll be amazed how much you learn if you can do this. Wednesday is your day off, and Saturday is busy with work, so that leaves five days for reading for an hour. On a Sunday, you're unlikely to want to read, so other study activity is better then, and Friday has a long gap in terms of unscheduled time, as does Tuesday, so better to spend two hours reading on a Friday and none on a Sunday. If we add reading to the timetable it might look something like Table 3.4.

Table 3.4

Time	Monday	Tuesday	Wednesday	Thursday	Friday	Saturday	Sunday
9–10			Lie in	Job at Tesco	Lecture 3	Job at Tesco	Lie in
10–11					Seminar 3		
11–12	Lecture 1		Shopping				Bar job
12–1		Seminar 2	Washing		Read journal article		
1–2			Lazy lunch				
2–3	Read journal article	Read journal article	Sports		Read book chapter		
3–4	Seminar 1				Lecture 4		
4–5	Seminar 4			Read textbook			
5–6		Lecture 2	Evening off socialising				
6–7	Bar job				Bar job		
7–8						Evening off socialising	
8–9							

Now you have five hours of allocated reading time in your week. Studying also involves discussing ideas and writing assignments. Discussing ideas is useful because we are generally social animals, and we can learn a lot from talking to each other. Often articulating an idea to another person helps us to clarify that idea for ourselves. We're also good at forgetting things, so reflecting on things helps us to learn them. It would be good then to start the week with a study group of a couple of friends and yourself discussing the week ahead, how you have prepared for it, and what reading you undertook last week. This could also be done at the end of the week, sometime on the Friday. If we add this to the timetable it looks like Table 3.5.

Table 3.5

Time	Monday	Tuesday	Wednesday	Thursday	Friday	Saturday	Sunday
9–10			Lie in	Job at Tesco	Lecture 3	Job at Tesco	Lie in
10–11	Study Group				Seminar 3		
11–12	Lecture 1		Shopping		Study Group		
12–1		Seminar 2	Washing		Read journal article		Bar job
1–2			Lazy lunch				
2–3	Read journal article	Read journal article	Sports		Read book chapter		
3–4	Seminar 1				Lecture 4		
4–5	Seminar 4			Read textbook			
5–6		Lecture 2	Evening off socialising				
6–7	Bar job				Bar job		
7–8						Evening off socialising	
8–9							

The study group review time could be carried out in the coffee shop and can be relatively informal, but the important thing is that you have an agenda and you stick to it. A typical agenda for a meeting might look something like this:

5 mins	Quick update on news and life
10 mins	Student 1 feeds back on reading from last week
10 mins	Student 2 feeds back on reading from last week
10 mins	Student 3 feeds back on reading from last week
10 mins	Discussion of relevance of reading to particular assignments
10 mins	Discussion of points of difficulty
5 mins	Consider the week ahead

The feeding back on reading from the previous week could take the form of sharing the database entries you have made, so that your study group can see what an article was about and discuss anything that is of interest. Your study group does not have to consist of people on your course, but it is best if they are studying something that is related to your course. So, for example, if you are studying Business Studies, your study group could have an Accounting student and an Economics student, but is unlikely to include a Biology student. You want your study group to consist of people who have similar interests and will be able to relate to what you are studying. If they are on the same course as you, you need to be careful to ensure that you all submit clearly different pieces of work for assignments, otherwise you might get accused of collusion which is an academic offence similar to plagiarism. The easy way to avoid this is to make sure you are on your own when you physically write your assignments. Chapter 4 discusses how best to learn from your peers.

FITTING ASSIGNMENTS INTO YOUR SCHEDULE

If there is one complaint that is common to all students on all courses, it is the timing of assignments. Every module is likely to want its assignment in at around about the same time. There is a very good reason for this. Academics like to give students as long as possible to work on their assignments – hence the deadline for submission is usually set backwards. The ultimate date that is immovable is the date of the exam board. Go back 2 weeks from that for sending the work to the external examiner. Go back 1–2 weeks from that for moderating within the institution. Go back 2–3 weeks from that for marking and you get the hand-in date. Modules that have smaller numbers of students can usually turn around assignments in the shorter timeframe, while large modules with hundreds of students need the extra time to co-ordinate the marking and moderating across more people.

Now, just because the hand-in date is towards the end of the module, that does not mean that you can't complete the assignment earlier than that – indeed you can usually hand it in earlier if you particularly want to, although it is safer to wait until the time actually due in case you want to improve it at all.

The assignment is also likely to include issues from the course that are not covered until later in the module, and hence to complete an assignment early you will need to read ahead of your lecture schedule in order to ensure that you have covered the additional material ahead of time. This is no bad thing at all as the lecture then serves as a form of revision and acts as a check on what you've already written in your assignment. If you wish you can also amend your assignment after the lecture to add additional points.

Let's say that you are studying four modules per semester, let's add 2 hours per week for each module for assignment preparation. This would mean that you are spending about 20 hours on each assignment in a 10 week semester. Your timetable now looks something like Table 3.6.

Table 3.6

Time	Monday	Tuesday	Wednesday	Thursday	Friday	Saturday	Sunday
9–10		Assignment module 2	Lie in	Job at Tesco	Lecture 3	Job at Tesco	Lie in
10–11	Study Group				Seminar 3		
11–12	Lecture 1	Read journal article	Shopping		Study Group		
12–1	Assignment module 1	Seminar 2	Washing		Read journal article		Bar job
1–2		Assignment module 3	Lazy lunch				
2–3	Read journal article		Sports		Read book chapter		
3–4	Seminar 1	Assignment module 4			Lecture 4		
4–5	Seminar 4			Read textbook			
5–6		Lecture 2	Evening off socialising				
6–7	Bar job				Bar job		
7–8						Evening off socialising	
8–9							

The final element you need to add to your timetable is preparation for the seminars. Usually an academic will ask you to read something or prepare something in advance of a seminar. Sunday evening could be a good time for this as you can take your time, and get yourself reading for the week ahead. You can also discuss this at your Monday morning study group. Tuesday is a good day as you can do some preparation in the morning, and review it in the evening (see Table 3.7). It is also good as it is part way through the week and hence lets you take stock of what has changed in the week so far.

Table 3.7

Time	Monday	Tuesday	Wednesday	Thursday	Friday	Saturday	Sunday
9–10		Seminar preparation	Lie in	Job at Tesco	Lecture 3	Job at Tesco	Lie in
10–11	Study Group				Seminar 3		
11–12	Lecture 1	Read journal article	Shopping		Study Group		
12–1	Assignment module 1	Seminar 2	Washing		Read journal article		Bar job
1–2		Assignment module 2	Lazy lunch				
2–3	Read journal article		Sports		Read book chapter		
3–4	Seminar 1	Assignment module 4			Lecture 4		
4–5	Seminar 4			Read textbook			
5–6		Lecture 2	Evening off socialising				Seminar preparation
6–7	Bar job			Assignment module 3	Bar job		
7–8		Seminar preparation				Evening off socialising	
8–9							

Now your week from 9am to 9pm consists of 29 hours of studying; 25 hours of working to earn money; 18 hours off; and 10 hours unscheduled – some of which will be taken up with travelling. This also allows you an extra 10 hours plus the hours after 9pm for panic writing of assignments nearer deadlines! However, if you stick to this type of timetable, you shouldn't be having that sort of panic.

Constructing your own timetable

Here is a blank timetable for you to complete for yourself. Make a copy of it so that you can do a new one each semester. Now lets fill it in.

Timetable for _____

Time	Monday	Tuesday	Wednesday	Thursday	Friday	Saturday	Sunday
9–10							
10–11							
11–12							
12–1							
1–2							
2–3							
3–4							
4–5							
5–6							
6–7							
7–8							
8–9							

1 Firstly enter your lectures and seminars, or any other classes at which you are expected to attend.

2 Second enter any job commitments you have to earn money – or any family commitments you are required to perform as a carer.

3 Next work out which day you can have as your complete day off – if this isn't possible, take two half days. Also try to give yourself an additional day on which you can lie in.

4 Now, let's start using up the 'free' time with studying activities. If you have a study group organised, add two meetings a week for the study group.

5 Add two hours per week (preferably together) for each assignment you need to write this semester.

6 Finally add one hour per week for 'pure reading' for each module you are studying, and four hours' worth of seminar preparation.

It should start to look quite full. If it isn't, maybe because you don't have to work as many hours as in the example, add an extra hour of reading time for each module as this will not go amiss.

In addition you could undertake useful 'voluntary' activities such as being an ambassador for your institution, which may involve you, for example, in going back to a local school once a week to work with children who are making choices about their future; or get involved in some other community project.

GETTING STARTED WITH BEING DISCIPLINED

It can be difficult to get going with such a disciplined approach. In your first week of the semester you are likely to have introductory lectures, and inductions to the facilities of the university. You may well spend a lot of time in queues getting your student ID card, your NUS card, a bus pass and so forth, so be patient. University staff work very hard in those first few weeks trying to get everybody up and running in a very short period of time. They may have upwards of 20,000 students to deal with in one week, so if it feels like you are a number in a production line, that is a little bit because you are – but for that week only!

The most important things to make sure you have at the end of your first week are your student ID card which gets you into the LRC and university network, and that you are enrolled on the correct modules for the semester. Once you are enrolled on the right modules, the academics know that you exist and will allocate you to seminar groups. The tutor who leads your seminar group should be your main point of contact for that module as they will get to know you best. The module tutor may be the person giving many of the lectures, but this may be to 500+ students, so they will not be able to know all 500 individually. For large modules, there are usually teaching teams to carry out the seminars, and they all have the same tasks to carry out. This means everyone is engaged in the same activities, it is just the tutor that may differ.

In your first lecture or seminar of the module you should be given your assignment for the module and some form of guided reading list. Some institutions may issue this electronically in advance so that students can download it and have a look through before attending so that they can have any questions or queries prepared. If your institution does offer this facility, have a look at everything you possibly can in advance as this helps you prepare and be in the right frame of mind when you attend.

Once you have your assignment and guided reading list, you can get started.

GETTING STARTED WITH ASSIGNMENTS

On your computer/laptop, make a separate folder for each module/assignment that you are working on. Ideally this is on your desktop so every time you start up your computer you see the folders, acting as a gentle reminder. Also it is easy to locate and save things into the folders if they are that prominent. Once you have completed an assignment you can move the folder off the desktop.

In the first couple of weeks of studying a module, your two hours of assignment time might be spent looking for specific evidence/reading that you can refer to in your assignment. This is a very valuable use of time, and if possible save the PDFs of the reading into your desktop folder. Remember also to write summaries of your reading into EndNote or some other form of electronic database as outlined in Chapter 2.

Have a separate word document called 'references' within this folder, and every time you read something or come across a quote or piece of data that is useful, record the reference in this document so that you don't have to go back and do it later on. Compiling reference lists retrospectively is very hard work. If you enter your reference in EndNote then also pull it through to this document so you know that you have used it already.

Once you have a few ideas about your assignment, start to write it in outline, or write a plan. This will show you where you have gaps that you need to fill and/or look for more evidence or reading to support your line of argument.

After a few weeks your assignment should be starting to take shape. You should have around 12 references that are relevant to the line of argument you are making, and some idea of the structure of the argument. You may also have drafted some of the text that you might use. Keep going with this process until you have the number of words required for submission. Then it is a case of going back over it and improving it as much as you can.

GETTING STARTED WITH READING

The handbook for your module should give you some form of guided reading list, even if it is just sources to look up. Most modules will refer you to one or a choice of core texts for the module. This will give you an overview of the course content and a basic understanding of what you need to know. There should also be some guidance as to what journals to read, either specific articles or relevant journal titles in the field. If it is the latter, then you need to skim over the contents pages of the journals (you can do this online) and select the articles that appear relevant to your learning and the line of argument you are making in your assignment. If it is the former, don't feel bound to stick to that list only. If you find the suggested articles are not addressing the line you want, do a search for some others. It may be wise to skim read these ones as well, so that you are sure you have covered them and can refer to them in passing in your assignment.

If there is an edited book on the list this is often the best place to start as each chapter in your database is a separate entry so you start to feel you are getting through lots of reading really quickly. For guidance on how to get the most out of reading, see Chapter 2.

GETTING STARTED WITH A STUDY GROUP

You are likely to find that the friends you make in the first couple of weeks at university change in the following month as people settle down into being their real selves. Finding the right people for a study group is quite difficult. You don't necessarily want these people to be the friends that you socialise with as it can be hard to focus on study issues with them, and you drift off into gossiping all the time.

Have a look around the people who are in your modules in the first week. Look for people who you think will engage in the idea of a study group and take it seriously. Ask them if they would like to form a study group that meets twice a week for an hour at a mutually convenient time just to talk through ideas. This is going to require some bravery on your part as it will mean approaching people who you haven't spoken to before. This is bound to feel a little scary – after all, what if they say no? The likelihood of them saying no is actually quite slim as everyone is in the same boat at university with nobody really knowing anyone else and everyone trying to find a new way of coping with the study routine. Hence most people you will ask are likely to say yes – that is why it is important to ask the right people. If possible, introduce as much diversity into the group as possible, so mix genders, ethnicity and age within the group – this is because it brings different perspectives to the conversation and makes the discussion more interesting and beneficial to all. If someone does turn you down – don't worry about it. It is their loss as they won't have a study group to belong to.

If people seem puzzled, wave this book at them and tell them that you're trying out an idea in it and would they like to give it a go. Point out to them that one of the key things that makes it work is that you are not best friends, but a group that comes together to study.

MANAGING STRESS THROUGH LOCUS OF CONTROL

One of the key causes of stress for students is running out of time to do their assignments. The other is exams but that is dealt with later in the book. If you manage your time well, you should have fewer problems with stress.

Think about it – running out of time leaves you feeling out of control. When you are out of control, you are powerless. The only way to regain control is to review whatever it is that is causing you stress in such a way that you can control it. This means you take the power back.

For example, you may think you are stressed because you don't have enough time to complete your assignment before it is due in. This is not something that you can do anything about, because there isn't enough time, and that is a fact. This could be reframed to 'I am stressed because I haven't left myself enough time in which to do this assignment'. Now you can do something about it. Firstly you can make sure that for the next assignment you leave yourself enough time by planning better. Secondly, you can work out what time you need and find ways of making the time – even if this involves going and talking to your tutor. You may, for example, have to take time off from your job, do some extra late nights of studying, miss a family lunch at the weekend, not go out for the week, and focus on getting your assignment done. The important thing is, you are back in control. Once you are back in control, you can manage the stress. If the reality is that you have not left enough time for two assignments and you are likely to fail both, then go and talk to the tutor of one of them and explain why you won't be submitting. You'll fail the assignment and have to resubmit. That is what would happen anyway if you hand in a very poor effort. You will, however, have doubled the time you have for the other assignment and hence have a better chance of passing the other module. That way you will only have one to resubmit.

It is important to remember that we always have choices – even if we don't like any of the choices that are open to us, there are always choices. Once you reframe something so that you are in control you open up the number of choices available to you.

Think about all the things that are causing you stress at the moment. List them below:

1 _____
2 _____
3 _____
4 _____
5 _____
6 _____
7 _____
8 _____
9 _____
10 _____

Now reframe these into sentences that give you control of where the stress is coming from. This may be a good activity for your first study group meeting as you will get to know each other and be able to help each other with this activity.

The difficult ones are when you are stressed because of the way that someone else is treating you. The way to rephrase that is that you are stressed because of the way that you are letting someone else treat you. Now the onus is back on you to control the way that you are letting someone else treat you. You can either change the way you let them treat you – i.e. deal with them and tell them it is not acceptable – or you can stop being stressed about it because you are choosing to let them treat you that way for the moment because it is easier than the other choices.

Can you see how everything can be reframed so that you have control? This links to an academic concept known as 'locus of control' which stems from attribution theory, originally attributed to Heider (1958). Attribution theory looks at the way in which people interpret the causes of behaviour. That is, do they think that a certain behaviour occurs because of something they do (i.e. internal forces) or because of something that is beyond their control (i.e. external forces)? If someone has an internal locus of control then they relate behaviour to their own personal attributes such as skill, ability, amount of effort, fatigue, state of mind, stress level and so forth. If someone has an external locus of control then they relate behaviour to environmental factors such as organisational rules and policies, the lecturers, the weather, their family, or other factors that are generally beyond their control.

Students with an internal locus of control can do very well – it is up to them. Students with an external locus of control will generally do badly as life happens to them rather than them taking control of it. Developing an internal locus of control is important if you are to manage stress and become disciplined in managing your study time. It will also help you take control of life more generally and be more successful in your future career.

There are always times when we are out of control and cannot help but get stuck, for example in a traffic jam when the motorway becomes a car-park for an hour and you have no option but to switch your engine off and wait for the obstruction ahead to be cleared. Even in these circumstances you can take back some of the control by having something with you to do in the event that you have time wasted. Carry a couple of articles in your car that are on your reading list and read them when you're stuck. This makes best use of dead time and you'll be surprised how much additional reading you get done.

THE DISCIPLINE AND ART OF LISTENING TO LECTURES

Potentially one of the most boring experiences at university is the lecture. This is when the academic generally stands at the front of the auditorium, and you, as one of maybe 250 students, are expected to listen to them for an hour. Many lecturers have come up with novel, entertaining ways of engaging you while you're there to make the whole experience more interactive, but there is a limit to what someone can do with a 1 to 250 ratio.

Most lecturers use some form of powerpoint presentation to help guide them through what they need to cover. It acts as a prompt to the lecturer. If you are able to have a printed copy of the powerpoint slides in advance of attending then that is best – take them to the lecture with you and annotate them with the examples and explanations the lecturer is giving. Otherwise you tend to spend most of the time copying down what is on the powerpoint and not listening to what is being said.

Lectures are generally not a very effective way of learning as it virtually impossible for anyone to concentrate for a whole hour on what someone else is saying. The average person can manage to concentrate for about 20 minutes before their mind starts to wander. Therefore there are good strategies that you can employ to help you listen in a lecture.

1 If the lecture notes/powerpoints are made available in advance, have a look at them in advance. This helps you get in the right frame of mind so you know what you are going to be listening to. Otherwise it is possible to spend much of the lecture trying to work out what it is supposed to be about.

2 Try to make some notes as the lecture progresses. These should be key points, and good examples if they particularly strike you. Examples are a good way of remembering theories and ideas.

3 If you find you are losing concentration then think about what has been said so far and write yourself a summary of a couple of sentences. Then start listening again.

4 Write down any questions that come into your mind as you are listening. These are things to read around later or to ask in your seminar. It shows you are listening and thinking about issues if you come up with further questions.

5 If the lecturer specifically points out something as important – write it down.

6 Don't panic if your mind has drifted. Don't try to copy the person next to you. Refocus and make notes again. Remember you are trying to note down the important messages from the lecturer, not absolutely everything that is said.

The whole purpose of making notes is to aid your learning. It is important to go back over them within a day of making them to make sure they make sense, and make them legible for future revision. Also going back over them should highlight the key questions or areas that you will want to read around further.

THE DISCIPLINE OF ATTENDING SEMINARS

The purpose of a seminar is to review and expand upon the content area of the lecture. Usually you have to do some preparatory work, often in the form of reading an article and critiquing it for discussion. You will get the most out of seminars if you do this.

Even if you have not had time to prepare for a seminar fully, you should still go along. Academics do get to know who attends and who chooses not to attend – and it is usually your choice – so it is important to establish a relationship with the tutor who takes your seminars. As the due date for assignments draws near or the exam approaches, academics are much more likely to give more time to students who have made the effort to attend throughout the year than they are to someone who is asking a question that they would have got the answer to had they bothered to turn up.

In many ways it is more important to attend the seminar than it is the lecture, although it can be difficult to put the seminar in context if you haven't been to the lecture. However, don't miss the seminar just because you missed the lecture.

Seminars are intended to be discussions facilitated by the tutor with the students asking questions and responding to each other, with the tutor taking on a guiding role. If nobody has done any preparatory reading then there isn't going to be much to discuss. Tutors are likely to be much more comfortable with, and used to, silence than you are. Not having prepared is therefore much more painful for the students than it is for the tutor.

Seminars are a means of embedding the learning concepts through employing a different learning methodology to the lecture. It is not a one-way delivery but a two-way or group conversation. It is your opportunity to raise some of the questions that you noted down as they occurred during the lecture. You can also test out ideas that you may have with the tutor, and get their advice on additional reading if you want to follow a specific line of interest.

Seminars are basically your best opportunity for getting one-to-one advice from your tutors. While most tutors run surgery hours, these aren't always convenient for you, and are often very busy so you only get five minutes of the tutor's time. Many of your peers will not take good advantage of the seminar process and hence there is likely to be time for you to use it to your own ends. Take advantage of the fact that you have a tutor present for a full hour and not many people in the room to share their time with.

CHAPTER SUMMARY

This chapter is your wake-up call on how difficult your life as a student is going to be if you are to do well. There isn't the time to hang out doing nothing, and you need to maintain focus and discipline throughout your student years. Use this time well and you will find that not only do you do well but you have learnt the skills necessary to be efficient and effective in the workplace also. Being a success at university is as much about discipline as it is about being clever.

BUSINESS GAME

The frozen food company is so pleased with your marketing report on Brazil that they send you out to Brazil for a month to establish networks and build a client base. They have hired a local agent and interpreter to work with you for the month. Outline below how you will spend the time over the month to maximise the opportunity for the company.

	Mon	Tues	Wed	Thurs	Fri	Sat	Sun
Week 1							
Week 2							
Week 3							
Week 4							

There will be various meetings that you need to fit into your month, but you will also want to visit a range of outlets that might be stocking the product, wholesalers, distributors, and get a feel for the competition. Spend some time at the weekend standing by the frozen food counters and watch what sort of people buy what sorts of foods. Who should you be aiming your products at? Get as much of a feel for the market as possible.

Reference

Heider, F. (1958) *The Psychology of Interpersonal Relations.* New York: John Wiley & Sons.

4 ▶ HOW TO LEARN FROM OTHERS

This chapter looks at group working and team working, and how to move from being a group to a team. Often you have to do group work while at university, sometimes in groups that are chosen by the faculty rather than yourselves. It is important to understand, therefore, why some groups work and some don't, and how to improve the situation for dysfunctional groups.

This chapter will cover:

- The difference between a group and a team
- Understanding group and team behaviour
- Ways of managing difficult group members

USING THIS CHAPTER

INTRODUCTION

Being disciplined about your studies does not mean being anti-social. You do not have to be sitting on your own at a computer terminal, reading, or writing in order to be studying and thinking. You could be engaged in a conversation that helps you learn, or undertaking group tasks. Human beings are essentially social animals – we tend to like to be with others – and more importantly, we learn from being with others. This chapter guides you on how to get the most out of being with others so that as well as being up to date with the gossip, you are also engaged in your studies and learning.

THEORY BEHIND GROUP LEARNING

One of the best known educational theorists is Vygotsky (1978) whose theory centres around what he calls the 'Zone of Proximal Development' or ZPD for short. Vygotsky believes that a person develops differently according to who they are with. Hence the people who are in their 'zone of proximal development' are the people who influence their development. This theory is tested every so often by experiments such as putting children from poor families into private boarding schools to see how they develop differently, but essentially the theory does suggest that who you learn with affects your learning.

On that basis, in order to get the broadest learning experience at university, you should try to have more than one group of people that you mix and learn with, hence expanding your ZPD, or indeed having more than one ZPD.

LEARNING FROM OTHERS

So how exactly do you learn from others? There are a number of ways of learning from others. Essentially you are looking to learn from their previous experiences so that the experience is shared. If someone else makes a mistake and they are prepared to share that learning with you then you don't need to make the same mistake as well. Equally if someone is very successful at something you will want to know what it is that they do to make them so successful. This is one reason why top sports people watch videos of other top sports people – to study what it is that they do and learn from that. You could argue that this is simply copying others, and to some degree it is, but as you copy someone doing something you have a new experience, and then as you repeat this you adapt it to your own style or ability and the outcome or experience changes.

Copying is one of the most established forms of learning that you will find in the workplace. Traditionally it was called 'sitting with Nellie' in factories, where new workers would sit with an experienced worker and watch what they did until they felt ready to copy it themselves. Then they would practise and have 'Nellie' oversee them to correct any mistakes, before finally developing their own expertise and adapting their style on their own.

There are many ways of developing the idea of 'copying' to help you with your studies. If you are having trouble writing, for example, it can be a useful exercise to read some writing that you like the style of out loud before you try to write yourself. This can get you into a rhythm which you can then continue (or copy) in your own writing. Hence you are not copying the words but the rhythm of the style.

LEARNING WITH OTHERS

If you make a mistake or fail something, sharing this experience with others can be a good way of recovering something from the failure. By discussing what you did and what went wrong, you reflect on the experience and note where the issues arose and how they can be avoided. That way you can learn how to do better next time. Equally, those people you are discussing the lack of success with can learn from you to help them avoid making similar mistakes in their work. Learning should not be a selfish process – it is a gift to share with others.

Learning can also occur through the sharing of new ideas and then sparking off against each other so that one idea leads to another and another in a form of 'brain-storming'. Brainstorming is when everyone shares their ideas on a topic and you just write them all down. Once everyone has run out of ideas you go back and revisit them all and go into detail discussing the merits and down-sides to the ideas noted. The idea behind brainstorming is that one person's idea makes others think about something they wouldn't have thought of on their own and then they come up with something, which again sparks off a new thought in a third person and so forth. The important thing with brainstorming is that you do not evaluate any of the ideas at the time they are mentioned – you go back and do that afterwards. Otherwise you are in danger of discarding the ideas that seem the most way out at the time but actually could be the best solution in the long term when considered later on.

It is always more enjoyable if learning is a positive experience, but you can equally learn loads from less than pleasant experiences of learning with others. Often this is learning about yourself, how you work with other people, what your strengths and weaknesses are, and what you like and dislike in other learners. Even if you are having a terrible time working with others, try to find something positive from the experience in terms of what you are learning and how you will take that learning forward to ensure you do not find yourself in the same position again.

GROUPS AND TEAMS

What is the difference between a group and a team – and why does it matter? A group is number of people who happen to be gathered in the same place and same time, and may or may not have a common purpose. For example, a crowd at a football match are a group with the common purpose of supporting their team; a group of people queuing for the cinema have a common purpose of wanting to see a film.

A team have more than a common purpose – they have a shared interest in the outcome. This then leads them to work together and become interdependent to achieve a common goal. Hence a football team work together to win the match.

At university you are likely to be involved in a number of groups and a number of teams. Groups will include seminar groups, social groups and sports groups to name but a few. You may also set up a study group which has a common purpose – to discuss learning – but no common goal in terms of a shared mark or assessment.

Think about all the groups that you belong to. List them below, identifying which are groups and which are teams. See if you can think of 10 of each – it is usually easier to identify groups than teams.

	Groups	Teams
1		
2		
3		
4		
5		
6		
7		
8		
9		
10		

Have you included your family at all? Do you see your family as a group or a team? There are some groups that will behave as teams on occasion but the rest of the time function as a group. Families are good examples of this. If there is a special occasion like a wedding or a surprise party, the family behaves as a team. The rest of the time, as they pass each other in the kitchen, they happen to be a group of people sharing the same facilities, and occasionally, possibly, sharing a meal together!

What about your friendship groups – are they behaving as groups or teams? As much as we'd like to think of our friends as a team, the reality is that we are usually behaving as groups.

Despite the fact that some assignments are called 'group assignments', they are actually team assignments and require you to work as a team. You will share the assignment submission and the mark given, and hence are interdependent and working to achieve a common goal.

Both groups and teams are discussed below to help you get the most out of both situations during your time at university.

ESTABLISHING A FORMAL STUDY GROUP

In Chapter 3 the idea of joining a study group was timetabled into the week for two single hour meetings a week. To get the most out of a formal study group, try to meet with people who are not really in your social group. The idea is that twice a week you meet for an hour to discuss issues arising from the lectures and your reading, or issues arising in your thoughts around your assignments. It is a meeting at which you share ideas and discuss points that you are struggling with.

The more diverse the study group, the better. You get the most out of a study group when people bring completely different views on the issue, apply ideas in different ways, and have different interpretations based on their different experiences and backgrounds.

Study groups should be a serious matter. Everyone should prepare and contribute and you need to be committed to your group members. Setting ground rules is important when you establish the group, and if group members don't stick to them, chuck them out of the group and replace them. Study groups only work if everyone is committed and keeps to the schedule. This is why it is best to have a study group which is not your best buddies, as you forgive each other when you are friends, and you need to be tough on each other in your study group – if you let the group down, you're out.

There is no absolute best number for a study group, but if you are fewer than three you are not really a group and if you have more than five then you will struggle to get round everyone in the time allowed. Hence four is probably the ideal as it also allows you to keep going if you need to chuck someone out of the group and replace them with someone else.

STUDY GROUP AGENDA

A typical study group agenda might look something like this:

5 mins	Quick update on news and life
10 mins	Student 1 feeds back on reading from last week
10 mins	Student 2 feeds back on reading from last week
10 mins	Student 3 feeds back on reading from last week
10 mins	Discussion of relevance of reading to particular assignments
10 mins	Discussion of points of difficulty
5 mins	Consider the week ahead

If there are four of you, obviously you will need to give time for four of you to feed back.

An alternative way of running the study group is that everyone agrees a question and then you think about the question for the next meeting where you can discuss the answer. This works better for some groups as the focus on reading doesn't meet everyone's needs. It really depends on the subjects you are studying, and the dynamics of the group and the personalities of the individuals.

If your study group has difficulty getting going, start by looking at key words or concepts and what these mean to you. Try to get to grips with the concepts listed in Chapter 1, such as validity and reliability with regard to your subject area and the reading that you are doing. For example, can a study ever be considered valid for drawing wider conclusions in the social sciences? How reliable can a test be, and what can you do to increase its reliability? These sorts of questions will help you get the conversation going and lead on to further questions for subsequent sessions.

GROUP WORK ASSIGNMENTS

Many courses now require that you complete assignments in groups. This is particularly the case in courses that involve an element of Business, as working in groups or teams is an everyday component of business life. Some courses will put you in groups, while others will allow you to self-select. Some will allocate the same mark to the whole group, while others have a mechanism for differentiating between group members.

It is unlikely that all group members will be of similar ability, and each group member is likely to have different skills and be able to contribute in different ways. It is important to get to know your group members at the start of the task so that you can play to people's strengths rather than trying to get everyone to do everything.

FORMING A TEAM

Getting started as a group can be difficult if you are put in a group and don't know any of the other members. Equally, even if you do know some of the others, you are unlikely to know everyone equally well. Tuckman and Jensen (1977) came up with a basic model of group formation and life-span that takes a group through five stages: forming, storming, norming, performing, and adjourning. Let's take each in turn, looking at what you can do to help the group through each stage of the process.

Forming

This is when the group first come together and get to know each other. You need to do some 'ice-breaking' exercises to help everyone get to know each other and start working together. You need to get to know each other's attitudes and personalities, backgrounds, strengths and weaknesses. Some ideas of exercises to help in this phase include:

- *Introducing each other* – spend 5 minutes in pairs telling each other about yourselves and then each pair has to introduce their partner to the rest of the group recalling as much as possible of what they found out in the 5 minutes.

- *If I was, I would be* – come up with a list of categories such as animals, colours, buildings, and so forth and go round the group answering the question 'if I was an animal, I would be a ???? because ...'. This is a really powerful exercise for understanding what people see as the key features of their personality as they will relate these to the reason for being the particular animal, colour, etc.

- *Human tangle* – this is one for groups of six or more; all stand in a circle, put your hands into the centre and grasp the hands of other people so that everyone is linked up. Now try to unravel the group so that you are all in big circle again without anyone letting go of hands. This is a good exercise for people who are feeling inhibited or not included as everyone has to take part.

- *Lower the pole* – find yourself a long stick, or a metre ruler or something like that. It should not be too thick or heavy, simply long and thin. Stand group members so that there are equal numbers each side of the stick. Everyone should hold out one finger on each hand and place this under the stick. Hence the stick is balanced on the fingers of every group member. Now lower the stick to the floor without anyone losing contact with the stick. This is remarkably difficult and often the stick rises before it lowers. The only way to achieve the task is to get into a sort of rhythm with each other.

- *Social event* – you could all go out for a social event together but make sure this is not based around alcohol as not everyone in the group might be comfortable with drinking for religious or personal reasons. Activities like bowling can be good for this.

Storming

As you get to know each other better you will start to feel more confident about challenging each other rather than agreeing with each other. This can be a bit uncomfortable at first and lead to some conflict. This is the time to set some ground rules as getting this right leads to highly productive groups, while failing to get through this stage leads to continual conflict and misery. Activities which help get through the storming phase include setting group ground rules so that there is agreement on how decisions will be made.

- *Ground rules* – these might include, for example: will you take votes or does everyone have to agree; will you set time limits on how long you will discuss matters or will you keep discussing something until there is agreement; how often will you report back on delegated tasks; how will you give feedback (some groups insist on everyone giving a positive piece of feedback and a constructive criticism on everything that everyone does so that everyone is treated equally and everyone gets both elements)?

- *Social event* – sometimes going out socially again can help ease the tension in this phase of team building as relationships can strengthen outside of the issues being discussed in the team.

- *Story telling* – if people are getting to a point that they are upset, the group could take some time out to tell stories. The story should be how the situation looks to them, how they perceive themselves as being treated, and how this makes them feel. Everyone needs to tell a story. Essentially you get a whole range of stories about the same situation and it allows the group to understand where people are at and how they are feeling. By getting this out in the open it allows other group members to modify their behaviour as they are unlikely to be wanting to have the negative impact that they are.

- *What's on top* – sometimes the conflict is related to things that are nothing to do with what is going on in the group but to other events that are happening to the group members. Taking some time out at the start of a team meeting just to say 'what is on top of your mind' gives other members the opportunity to empathise with where you are coming from. If, for example, someone's had some bad news or is particularly stressed about an incident that occurred earlier in the day, the group will understand that their lack of engagement with them might not actually be to do with them at all, and hence 50 per cent effort from that person on that particular occasion might suffice.

Norming

This is where the group settles down and starts to apply its own ground rules and find the acceptable way of working. Some groups can oscillate between storming and norming for a while and that almost becomes part of the norming process. This phase is about becoming comfortable about the way you are working. Meetings start to take less time to get more done, and the awkwardness that can surround group formation disappears.

Performing

Now your group is really starting to motor and make progress on the task at hand. This is where you can really start focusing on the group assignment, delegating tasks between the group, feeding back and commenting on each other's contribution. This is where tasks get handed from person to person with each one building on the previous person's efforts. People feel secure enough to let others change their work without taking it as personal criticism. If you are working online, this is similar to a Wiki way of working, where everyone can access, change and add to the same document. Although it is tempting for the group to progress with the assignment from the day you first get together, you will be most productive if you start the assignment once you reach this part of the group formation process. If you have started it already, take some time out and go back to the beginning to see if you would change anything to make it better rather than settling for what was produced initially in the forming, storming and norming phases.

Adjourning

It is unusual for groups to stay together throughout the whole of your course. Different modules might place you in different groups; people will choose to leave groups or the course; new people will join. This phase can see some change of membership in the group or the complete dissolution of the group. This is a good time to draw out learning from the experience and a team should have one final meeting after the assignment is handed in to reflect on what they did well, what could have been improved, and how they would work differently if they were to do it again.

This framework helps you through the process of the group's life. Other theories look at the membership of groups and what you need in order to establish the perfect team. There are various team theories that might help you understand how to get the best from each different team member. Perhaps one of the best known is that of Meredith Belbin.

BELBIN'S TEAM ROLES

Belbin outlines nine different team roles that need to be present in a team in order for the team to function optimally as a 'winning team'. This does not mean that you need to have nine people in the team as each person is likely to fulfil more than one role. Neither does every team have to cover all nine, nor does that stop them from being productive. However, if all nine are covered, then optimum performance is likely to be achieved. Each team role adds a different contribution to the team, but

Table 4.1 **Belbin's team roles**

Role and description of contribution	Allowable weakness
Plant: This is the problem solver who is creative, generates ideas, and 'thinks outside the box'.	Doesn't always think of all the detailed implications; not always an effective communicator.
Resource investigator: This is the person who runs around sourcing information and resources through their extroverted personality.	Can lose enthusiasm after initial push.
Co-ordinator: This is the conductor in the group who is a good chair and delegator, communicating well and ensuring everyone knows what they are doing.	Doesn't always do much themselves as they co-ordinate rather than do.
Shaper: This is the person who drives the group and finds ways to overcome obstacles to achieve the task.	Doesn't always consider other people's feelings in their task focus.
Monitor evaluator: This is the person who tends to sit quietly, listening and weighing up what is going on, who then delivers their opinion in a very measured way.	Can be seen as over-critical and not excited by the task.
Teamworker: This is the person who makes sure the shaper and monitor evaluator, in particular, don't kill each other. They maintain good working relationships in the group.	Can be easily influenced and lacks decision-making ability.
Implementer: This is the person who turns the plant's ideas into actions in a disciplined, rigorous and efficient manner.	Can lack adaptability to change and appear rigid in their thinking.
Completer: This is the person who proof-reads and double-checks everything, and ensures all is done on time to the required standard.	Can worry too much and cause stress by their lack of ability to delegate.
Specialist: This is the expert who is sometimes needed. They are dedicated to their knowledge and expertise. Not every team needs this role.	Contribution is in a limited area. They are only focused on their narrow element and tend not to be interested in the bigger picture.

Source: Adapted from Belbin (1993) *Team Roles at Work.*

with that comes an 'allowable weakness' which is in essence the dark side of the strength. Often conflict arises in teams because the different team roles are viewing the same thing from different perspectives. The nine team roles and their allowable weaknesses are outlined in Table 4.1.

One of the most useful things about Belbin's team roles is that if you are put into a group with people and find that someone is driving you mad and is really difficult to work with, usually you can identify why that is by looking at the team roles. For example, the 'monitor evaluator' in the team can be incredibly frustrating to work with as they will sit quietly looking like they are not contributing when in reality they are listening intently and weighing things up, and then just when a decision is made and everyone is keen to get going, they will undermine the decision with a cata-strophic evaluation that makes you feel like you've just wasted the last hour of discussion. However, once you appreciate that is how that role operates, you can involve that person sooner by drawing out their thoughts earlier in the discussion, and temper your emotional response because you can now understand that they are not being deliberately difficult.

Think about people you have worked with in the past. Can you identify which team roles they took when they were working with you? Can you identify your own team role(s)?

EXPELLING THE TEAM MEMBER WHO DOESN'T PERFORM

Whatever the format of group selection (imposed or self-selected), the biggest problem that people have with group work assignments is that sometimes one or two members of the group don't pull their weight and one or two others have to do extra to compensate.

This is all part of the group work experience. If you are one of the people who are carrying others, you need to find strategies for engaging the 'lazy' members to pull their weight. People who are not being fair to the group are unlikely to be feeling bad about this, or wasting energy on it – while you, on the other hand, will be wasting a lot of energy. If they were feeling bad, they would do something about it. Also, they are likely to offer external factors as excuses for their lack of production so that it is never 'their fault' that they haven't done their bit. This links back to the locus of control discussed in Chapter 3.

There is only one thing that ultimately makes poor group members perform and that is expulsion from the group. Obviously you can't just chuck them out of the group the first time they let you down, you need to give them some warning and draw up an agreed plan for their contribution. If they then fail to meet that plan, speak to your tutor and tell them what you are planning to do. Your tutor may try talking to the student for you so that they know how serious this is. If they still don't engage and make an effort, then chuck them out of the group. They will now be in a position where they don't have a group to do the group work assignment and will either have to negotiate access to another group or do the whole assignment on their own. You, on the other hand, will have one group member less but not the hassle, waste of energy or emotion, or hold-ups of a non-performer and can reassign their element among those remaining and complete the task. Make sure you make your tutor aware of the situation before you chuck the group member out – the process has to be fair, so the non-performer must have time and opportunity to redress their poor performance. This is much like disciplinary procedures in the workplace – two verbal warnings, a written warning and then you're out!

This action is not likely to leave you popular with some people in your class but this should not deter you from doing it. Firstly, others can take the poor performer into their group if they choose – which they won't; and secondly, if people think worse of you for it, they're unlikely to be the sort of people you want to be friends with anyway.

VIRTUAL TEAM WORKING

Most students now are dependent on their laptops/computers. Indeed many switch on their laptop first thing in the morning – even on the way to the toilet rather than on the way back! The laptop is your salvation for information, communication, your work and keeping in touch with friends. Given this, you might find it easier or preferable to undertake your group work virtually. This is absolutely fine, and indeed can benefit the group work process as it is asynchronous, and hence not everyone has to be available at the same time.

The same rules, however, do still apply, and it may be worth having one face-to-face meeting to cover the ice-breakers and setting the ground rules – although these can be achieved online. There are endless possibilities for group activities online: you could create avatars in Second Life, for example, and go to social events together as your avatars; you could engage in group game sites; you could have a discussion board where you exchange ideas; you could create a Wiki document that you can all work on at the same time. The best thing is, though, that you don't all have to be online at exactly the same time if it is not possible – everyone can make a contribution at some point during a 24-hour time period so that when the first person logs back on the next day, they can see the contribution of others.

This freedom with time is beneficial to groups for a number of reasons. Firstly, there is the obvious difficulty of everyone being available at exactly the same time in the same place for a face-to-face meeting. Secondly, is the increase in inclusivity –

some group members may, for example, not have English as their first language and hence find it difficult to keep up with and contribute to a meeting in English as the pace is quicker than an online discussion where they can take their time to digest matters. Third is the removal of emotion – when matters get heated in a face-to-face meeting, response can come thick and fast. In an online environment, everyone has time to reflect and think before responding so the instant hot-headed reply can be avoided. Finally, the non-attender might remain in attendance. Often the person that you want to expel from a group is better at attending online. Often they are someone who is too weak a personality to say no to their friends and hence miss a meeting to be sociable and maintain an image as a socialite when actually they do want to make a contribution and will do so when they are at home alone – even if it is at 4am!

Virtual teams also seem to go through less of a storming phase, probably because much of the personality element is tempered down through the written communication process rather than oral communication.

INFORMAL GROUPS AND SOCIAL LEARNING

Some students find the social opportunities at university great and take as many opportunities to party and go out as possible. This isn't for everyone so don't worry if you don't do this but prefer to engage in other activities. However, if you are the budding socialite it is important to get the most from social situations also. This is not to say that you have to talk about your studies all the time, but if there is something that you are pondering, some deep philosophical question that is underpinning your thoughts, then often it makes for good discussion in the pub. After a beer or two, people drop a lot of their inhibitions and you are much more likely to get them to express their deeper feelings on a subject in this sort of situation than in a classroom with a tutor present. The sorts of points that you might want to discuss are those almost taken for granted assumptions that you don't really have the opportunity to challenge. For example:

- Is the equal opportunities movement really about achieving equality and social justice, or is it just people paying lip-service to an idea to stop them feeling guilty about having a social advantage?
- Is there really such a thing as free market economics or is every market controlled by the most powerful players?
- Who decides what should be included in 'the news'? What is happening in the world that we don't know about?
- Is the law really about seeking justice?
- Who controls the internet, and/or should it be controlled?
- Has global warming reached a point that the planet is now unsustainable?

If you want, you could even set a question in advance for thinking about before you get to the pub – not for reading up on, just for thinking about. This sort of activity is about developing your mental agility and ability to reason orally, although too many beers and the latter might not happen!

CHAPTER SUMMARY

This chapter has introduced you to some ideas of how best to work in groups and learn from and with other people. This has to be a social activity in that you have to communicate, but it does not have to be done face to face. Virtual group learning can be highly effective and of very high quality as group members have more time to consider their responses before offering them to the rest of the group. If you find yourself assigned to a group which is really not working, do something about it. Either get yourself reassigned to another group, or expel the member(s) who are not working or pulling their weight – but make sure you talk to your tutor first. Group work is one of those things that people either love or hate. Some people prefer it to individual work, others don't. Either way, this chapter offers some explanations as to why groups work the way they do to help you understand what is happening and how you can improve matters.

BUSINESS GAME

Your return from your month in Brazil is a bit of an anti-climax as there is no obvious role for you back in the company, although they assure you that your job is secure. Their biggest UK customer is holding a charity competition event and your boss has entered a team from your company. As you have time to spare, you have been given the job of building the team for the charity competition. The company has booked for you to take a further eight people to the National Watersports Centre for a three day team-building experience. You can't swim and are terrified of water but have never told anyone this in your company. How do you go about approaching the three days?

Day 1: _____

_____

_____

Day 2: _____

_____

_____

Day 3: _____

_____

_____

Team building is always good fun and can also go horribly wrong. Perhaps day 1 should be spent getting to know each other and what you can contribute to the team. Look at each other's strengths and weaknesses, and what your team roles are. This should surface your fear of water and if this is done well the team will support you in your role as co-ordinator and coach rather than contributor within the water. Then it is about developing activities to get the team working together. Much of the success of these depends on how you feed back to the team on how they are progressing.

References

Belbin, M. (1993) *Team Roles at Work.* Oxford: Butterworth Heinemann.

Tuckman, B. & Jensen, N. (1977) Stages of small group development revisited. *Group and Organizational Studies*, 2, 419–427.

Vygotsky, L. S. (1978) *Mind in Society.* Cambridge, MA: Harvard University Press.

5 ▶ HOW TO DEAL WITH STUDY DEPRESSION

This chapter is the one to read when everything is too much for you and you are feeling down about being at university. There is an old adage that 'university is the best days of your life', but this isn't true for a lot of students. It is important to understand that you are not alone if you are not enjoying your time at university and there are support mechanisms in place to help you through your time at university.

This chapter will cover:

- Why you might be feeling down when at university
- Where to go for support and help
- Strategies to help you get through your years at university

USING THIS CHAPTER

If you want to dip into this section	Page	If you want to try the activities	Page
The difficulty of self discovery	78	Dietary diary	75
Myths about university	78–9	Business game	85
Points of support	81–2		

INTRODUCTION

This chapter will discuss surviving life at university, common difficulties faced in settling in, leaving home, not leaving home, and needing to work, manage finances and being generally poor and miserable! Particular focus will be on how to manage the depression that sets in when you feel you don't understand anything, don't know where to start, can't write an essay, don't know what's expected, or feel like you are failing.

WHAT IS STUDY DEPRESSION?

Some people reading this chapter will be wondering what it's about as you haven't reached the point yet where study depression has set in. Hopefully, it won't. For others of you, this may have started in week 1 as you battle with the fact that you hate being at university but you're sufficiently motivated to get the degree at the end of it that you are determined to stick it out. For others still, this chapter might be relevant part way through your course. It is unlikely that this chapter won't be relevant to most students at some point in their studies as there are going to be highs and lows over the three-year period. This chapter tries to offer you some support when you are in a low.

This is not an official medical illness or condition at all, although clinical depression may occur at the same time and you may be advised to consult your doctor if you are feeling particularly low. Study depression is when you wake up in the morning and realise that you hate your studies; you hate being a student; you hate your subject area; you hate the university; you hate the other students; and you don't want to be a student anymore. Unfortunately, unless you drop out, you're stuck with it for the remainder of your course. It is this feature that I think makes study depression different from other forms of depression – you are only stuck with it for the remainder of your course. There is a time limit; an end in sight; a final day when you know it will all be over; a light at the end of the tunnel.

HEALTH AND WELL-BEING

One reason that your mental health is likely to suffer at university is because your physical health is likely to also. Firstly, you are coming into a new environment with hundreds of other strangers, all of whom bring different germs from different parts of the country, and hence universities are literally breeding grounds for viruses. This doesn't just affect the students – note how many lecturers go off sick approximately 6–8 weeks into the first term with flu or other types of virus. Our immune systems

build up over time to fight the bugs and germs that are local to our common environment. When we go to university, we are in a brand new environment and hence our immune systems meet new bugs and germs and take time to adjust.

Secondly, you're unlikely to have a well balanced diet while you are university if for no other reason than cost. It is much more expensive to eat healthily than it is to eat unhealthily, and hence most students find it difficult to maintain a balanced diet while they are studying. This further weakens your immune system and leaves you susceptible to illness.

Keep a diary of what you eat for a week. Try to make one change a week to improve the balance of your diet.

	Monday	Tuesday	Wednesday	Thursday	Friday	Saturday	Sunday
Breakfast							
Lunch							
Dinner							
CHANGE							
Alcohol							

Third is change in lifestyle. Many students find they are staying up later, sleeping less and drinking more than they were previously. This also impacts on your immune system as you do not give your body time to recover properly. In addition, alcohol is a depressant. Keep a note of how much you drink, as you may be surprised when you see it written down.

STUDYING AWAY FROM HOME

Students living at home benefit here as they don't have the change in living conditions that those studying away experience, but most students living away from home find that their accommodation is far from the standard they are used to,

particularly in terms of dampness and the cold. Heating is an expensive luxury for many students, and dampness pervades as a result of this. This further weakens your immune system, and also is pretty miserable in itself – nobody enjoys being cold.

In addition, you have to learn to fend for yourself, which means shopping, laundry and all those other necessities of living that just seemed to happen when you lived at home. Actually planning shopping for the week can be difficult for some as you don't know what you'll want to eat, so bread, potatoes and baked beans become the staple diet for many. Invariably you need to share a fridge with other people, so there isn't the room to store fresh produce for the whole week. Practicalities like that lead to a poor diet and impact on your well-being. Keeping a shopping list might feel like the sort of thing that 'old people' do, but actually it will save you a lot of time and free up your memory for your studies. Make a list of things you need to buy as you think of them, and then try to shop once a week only.

For those living away from home there is also the issue of home-sickness. There is bound to be a time when you simply miss what you remember as the comforts of the home you came from, whether that is in terms of family, friends, or your home itself, there is likely to be a time when you just want to go back and miss it more than anything, to the point that it is all you can think about. However, if you were to go back – and maybe you should for a couple of days – you'll find that while home hasn't changed, you have, and actually you want more than that now.

STUDYING WHILE LIVING AT HOME

For those living at home, there is bound to be a time when you want to move on and you feel like everything around you is holding you back. This is the reality of studying – you will move on, and those around will not. Somehow you have to find a way of coming to terms with that, and forgive those around you for not moving on with you, because that is the source of the frustration.

Although it is about a mature student, the film/book called *Educating Rita* offers a lovely view of this phenomena, where a woman decides to go and better herself and get an education, and her husband and family find it difficult to accept how that process is changing her as a person.

ESTABLISHING A FRIENDSHIP GROUP

In your first weeks of university everyone is in the same boat – nobody knows anyone else and everyone is trying to make friends. People project themselves in their best light, and the fear that you won't meet anyone else you like tends to make

you stick to early acquaintances that really you have nothing in common with. As you get to the end of the first month, you're likely to start really getting to know people as it is difficult to keep any falseness going for a prolonged period of time. You start to see what people are really like, and often you start to find that you don't really like them, and don't really have anything in common with them.

Hence at the end of the first month, there tends to be a bit of a shift round again of friendship groups. So who do you regroup with?

Firstly, look around your seminar groups and try to find people who you think have a similar work ethic to yourself. These are people who you are likely to be able to talk to about your study process, and they are likely to feel similarly to you as you progress through the course.

Secondly, look to join some societies at the fresher's fair which genuinely appeal to you. Don't just join the societies that you feel you should join – choose some where you think you will find like-minded people, even if they seem a little way out and unfashionable at the time. University is an opportunity for you to define who you are, so take some risks and try some opportunities that are unlikely to be available later on in your life.

ADDITIONAL ANGST FOR INTERNATIONAL STUDENTS

As well as all the issues that home students have, overseas students have the added difficulty that they are in a foreign country, with a different diet, pace and way of life, and often a different first language. Overseas students face additional difficulties and hence tend to find the best support available to them is their peer group of other foreign students. This is why international students tend to stick to groups within themselves. True integration of overseas students into UK university culture is rare but can occur. It means that overseas students are invited to join study groups; their culture is acknowledged with regard to the social activities that are undertaken; their diet is catered for; and the local community welcomes them into their midst. This is not the usual experience for overseas students and hence they have added difficulties to overcome in their studies.

If you are reading this as an international student, try to establish contact with the local community that best represents your heritage. Use the international office at the university as an additional support mechanism as they will be able to give you advice on how to survive in the UK.

THE DIFFICULTY OF SELF-DISCOVERY

There is something about undergraduate study in particular that can leave you at a very vulnerable point, because you start to change and move on to something new – even if you don't know what that is yet – but everything around you stays where it was, and it is like you leave it behind. The trip home when you realise that your old mates in the pub are having the same conversation they were having when you last saw them eight months ago, and the world has moved on since them, but they haven't. The conversation with your parents when you realise that they are in a routine of life that leads them to do the same pattern of things every day and they continue in that cycle indefinitely – and while you've stepped off the cycle, the wheel simply carries on rotating without you. This is a very scary place to be, as suddenly you don't feel like you belong anywhere – but you will. This is a point of self-discovery that is the essence of the university experience – it is about learning, and learning about yourself. At this point you have choices to make about who you want to be, and what you want to aspire to. If you decide it is the person in the pub back home, then fine. If it is stepping back on to the cycle of family life, then fine. But it doesn't have to be. There is no right answer here – it is simply your choice – and while you are making this choice, study depression can hit hard as it is not a comfortable place to be at all.

This leads us to a number of myths about university that need to be dispelled right away:

Myth 1: University is the best years of your life

There is a popular myth that you will no doubt have heard, if not from family then from teachers, friends, or work colleagues, and that is 'that your student days are the best years of your life'. If you're reading this six months into your course and are completely miserable and wishing you'd never started your course then trust me – the myth is just a myth, and life gets a whole lot better once you've finished. The myth has its roots in a historical ideal of a university, when less than 10 per cent of the population went to university and they were largely from the upper classes. The myth was generated by students who didn't have any financial worries or concerns when they were students; they didn't have to work to earn money to sustain themselves; they didn't have to contribute to the family income; and they didn't have to watch how much they spent because money was not an issue for them. While everybody would hope that students do enjoy themselves at university, it is very unlikely in this day and age that your university years are going to be the best years of your life, so don't get too depressed if you're not enjoying yourself – it gets better once you've finished.

Myth 2: Studying is easy compared to 'real work'

Anyone who says this is unlikely to have been to university, and if they did go, they probably went a long time ago and can't remember what it was like – or have no idea what it is like now. They are also likely to be jealous of the fact that you are studying and they are not. Studying is not easy. It requires self-discipline, focus, cognitive skills, learning, writing skills, communication skills and team working. How many people need to use all of those every day in their work? Most would fall at the first hurdle – self-discipline – as the workplace is highly structured and monitored so that you aren't reliant on self-discipline. That is the role of supervisors and managers, roles that do not exist for students. 'Real work' can also be difficult, but it requires a different skills set and routine to studying so the two should not really be compared. Also, many students do also do 'real work' as they need to have part-time jobs to help support their studies. So, if you're getting hassle from people who are telling you that what you're doing is easy – they haven't a clue, so forgive them for that, let them think what they want, don't waste your energy on the argument, and move the conversation forwards. Nobody can argue with you if you agree with them.

Myth 3: You'll meet your best friends and husband/wife/partner at university

While university does offer you the opportunity to meet a whole new population of people, why on earth should one of them be your future spouse? Indeed, why should you like everyone or even anyone that is there? This is back to the group and team issue. University is full of other people who have the same purpose as you – to get a degree. That's it. That is all you share in common. There is nothing to say that you should like anyone, have anything in common with anyone, never mind fall in love with anyone. This is a complete myth. Don't worry if you are finding that you don't like your fellow students – why should you? You probably don't have much in common with them other than the desire to get a degree.

MANAGING FINANCES

One of the biggest causes of stress among the student population is debt. This should not actually be surprising as it is one of the main causes of stress for any adult who finds themselves in a position of debt, so why should it be any different for students? The difference is that students are almost expected to be in debt. There are fees that need to be paid for which a loan can be obtained. If you are a UK student there are actually a wide range of grants and financial incentives that can be drawn down to contribute to fees but not many people know about them. Check out the website of the university you are applying to and don't feel bad about applying for a bursary or grant – think of them as a way of the government trying to redress the imbalance they have caused by introducing fees in the first place.

MANAGING LONELINESS

The nature of university study makes it a very lonely experience compared to other study experiences you might have had previously. There isn't the tutorial support that you find in schools. There isn't the security of having the same group of friends in every class. The focus is on developing you as an independent learner, so much of the security of instruction has disappeared. The university buildings are big, compared to school or college, and they are full of unfamiliar faces that you don't know. It is easy in these circumstances, despite the fact that there are loads of people around you, to feel desperately lonely.

This is where initiatives such as having a study group can really help you, as they ensure that you do have people to talk to and discuss matters with, ensuring that at least twice a week you feel more included. Sometimes phoning home can add to the sense of loneliness and isolation and hence is not always the best strategy. What you need to do is find someone who you can really talk to, engage in a proper conversation rather than small talk, and reduce your feeling of isolation.

MANAGING FAILURE

Students fear failure more than anything else at university, and this is understandable as the whole point of your being there is to pass your degree. However, fear in itself can be a limiting factor as it can hinder your mental processes and performance. Fear of failure is based on a fear that we can't handle what is going to come our way. A little trust in ourselves and our abilities, and this fear goes away. Much has been achieved with sports psychologists to help athletes perform in competition – similar techniques can be used in your studies to help you believe in yourself and that you can handle what is coming your way.

There are likely to be times during the course of your studies that you don't achieve the results that you are hoping for or expect. Even if the results are okay and technically a 'pass', they may feel like failure to you. Alternatively, they may actually classify as failures and you will need to resubmit an assignment or retake an examination. This can be very hard to recover from, but you must. First of all, go and speak to your tutor about exactly what you needed to do to get a better grade. Ask if you can see a copy of an assignment that was top of the range so you have a model against which to compare – they may not be able to show you this, but they might. Students find it enormously helpful to see examples of excellent work as then they know what is expected of them.

It is important that you keep the failure in perspective. It is not you that is the failure – it is the piece of work that you submitted that failed – so don't take it personally.

Keep it in perspective and reframe it as a positive. Failing early on allows you to learn more and gain greater success later.

Also, don't feel guilty about recovering from the knock and doing better than expected in future. You are that good – you just made a mistake with that particular assessment.

SUPPORT POINTS

Support point 1 – do not drop out; inter-collate!

If you have really bad study depression, and the end of the course seems too distant a timeframe, pull in the timeframe to the end of the module. Once you get to the end of the module you can take a measure of whether or not you feel able to go on to the next module or if you need a break. DO NOT DROP OUT. There is an administrative process in a university called 'inter-collating' which most people are not aware of. This is a process that literally suspends your studies for a semester or year as is appropriate to your course, allowing you some time out to get yourself together to decide if you want to come back or not. Nothing changes during this time – everything is simply put on hold. If you choose not to come back, you can then claim a certificate for whatever credits you have accrued over your period of study until you stepped out. If you decide to come back, you simply pick up and carry on, but obviously with the next cohort of students as your cohort will have continued on without you. Some universities require a doctor's certificate to process an inter-collation, but if you are feeling so down that you are considering dropping out, you will probably find a doctor sympathetic to your needs and they should be willing to provide you with the certificate you require.

Support point 2 – student counselling services

Do not be afraid of going to use the counselling services – this is not a sign of weakness, but rather a sign of strength. Realising that you are struggling and need to talk things through with someone is a huge step in the direction of being able to resolve some of the issues you are struggling with. Sometimes just being able to share with someone else how utterly miserable you are feeling can be enough to start you feeling better as it somehow helps lessen the burden. Some universities appreciate that students don't like to be 'seen' to be going for counselling and hence offer online counselling or a counselling service in Second Life.

Support point 3 – study skills support

Most universities will have some form of study skills support for students who are struggling with essay writing, exams or more generally with the study pattern at university. Do not feel stupid if you need to access these services. The fact that you are reading this chapter suggests that these services could benefit you. You would be more of a fool not to ask for help than to recognise you are struggling and seek some advice. Nobody gets behind the wheel of a car and drives perfectly first time – we need instruction and help to hone our skills and pass our driving test. The same is true for studying – don't expect to be able to do it perfectly from the start; get some help (such as reading this book, or study skills support) and improve your performance.

The fact that most universities provide this support service gives you an indication of how widespread the need is for this form of support. If you are struggling with one type of study skill in particular, go and seek help.

Support point 4 – LRC staff

The people that staff the learning resource centre are not simply there to sign out books and collect fines for late return; they are subject specialists who know more about searching for information than we are ever likely to know. That is their profession – they are specialists at it. If you are therefore struggling with finding data, resources, or refining search terms in databases, ask them for help. They will be delighted to use their skills to help you rather than collect your fines, and they are a much underrated resource in universities. Successful students realise this and utilise them to the maximum, getting them to give some guidance on sources of information every time they start a new assignment.

Support point 5 – sports groups

One thing that is usually good regardless of which university you are at is the sports facilities. Sports can be a really good way of meeting people with a common interest that aren't necessarily studying for your course. Sports also help you release endorphins which are a natural mood booster which is why exercise can make you feel better. Sports also ensure that you are focusing your brain on something completely different which can shift the focus away from the loneliness or depression that might be lingering.

DEVELOPING A POSITIVE MENTAL ATTITUDE

Attitude is a very sensitive area. It is close to your ego and your identity. Nobody likes to be told to change their attitude – however, if you are feeling low and depressed, you need to develop a positive mental attitude. Your attitude is the way that you look at the world; it is how you look at your environment and your future; it is the focus you develop towards life itself. There are a number of points of advice that students have been given over the years that might help you feel better:

- You can take the pictures of life that you want to take. The optimist proclaims that we live in the best of all possible worlds, and the pessimist fears this is true. Keep your focus on the fact that your studies have an end point so you are creating a picture for a fixed period of time.

- Everyone has both positive and negative factors in their life. Positive people manage to redefine the negatives to find a positive within them. So for example if you fail an assignment, you have the benefit of some early learning so that you can improve rather than failing later on.

- You cannot eliminate the negatives, but you can concentrate more on the positives. If the grass is greener in the other fellow's yard, let him worry about cutting it. Don't compare yourself too much to others. Your time at university is about you, not you against anyone else. Everyone can achieve a first class degree if they are good enough – it is not a competition.

- Refuse to worry about the negative elements in your life that you can do nothing about. If you are powerless to change some things, then don't waste your energy on them. Move on, accept them and concentrate your energy on things you can do something about.

- Do not borrow negative factors from other people by trying to live their lives for them. Some people can become a drain on you. While you obviously don't want to be unsympathetic to friends, do not let them become too influential on you. You choose to give them as much time and support as you want, but make sure you feel in control of it.

- Dispose of small nagging problems quickly by addressing them. Take care of bigger problems by breaking them into smaller components that can be solved. Don't let anything become so big that it is too much to deal with.

- When anticipating what lies ahead, think about the good things that can happen. Things turn out best for people who make the best of the way things turn out. Focus on what success looks like rather than the minimum you have to do to avoid failure.

- When replaying the events of a day, think about your accomplishments. It is good to reflect on your learning and achievements at the end of every day as often we don't embed our learning. Even if learning has occurred from negative incidents, this is the time to think about them positively in terms of how they have contributed to your day, your learning, and your broader development.

- Don't take one day at a time – live one day at a time. Most people's tombstones should read: Died at 30, Buried at 60. Your time at university really is an opportunity for you to consider your future, what you want to achieve, and how you want to achieve it. It is an opportunity for laying foundations, and for changing the path that people might be expecting you to take. Even if you are hating the experience, appreciate it for what it is and focus on the end game.

■ University should not be a 35-hour weekly penalty, or something to endure. It should be a place where people feel good about themselves and their performance – a place where positive attitudes find expression. If you are feeling that it is a penalty, then focus on what it is that makes you feel good about yourself and draw that into your university experience. This may be sports, community work, supporting others or in some other area than studying.

There are certain phrases that we rely on when things aren't necessarily going the way we want them to be going. These can be rephrased into positive alternatives. The positive alternative gives you back your control so that you can do something about the negativity, rather than letting it depress you.

NEGATIVE	POSITIVE ALTERNATIVE
I can't	I won't
I should	I could
It's not my fault	I'm totally responsible
It's a problem	It's an opportunity
I'm never satisfied	I want to grow and learn
Life's a struggle	Life's an adventure
I hope	I know
If only	Next time
What will I do?	I know I can handle it
It's terrible	It's a learning experience

CHAPTER SUMMARY

This chapter is not meant to be a self-help guide to depression, nor is it a substitute for going to the doctor. It simply offers you some advice and ideas for dealing with the lows that occur when you are a student – and also lets you know that you are not alone in feeling this way. Trying to remain positive all the time is very difficult during your student years and it is not a sign of failure to ask for help, to talk to a counsellor, or even to visit your doctor. Make best use of the facilities to support you when you need them – that is what they are there for.

BUSINESS GAME

You've not had a good week. The Brazilian market for frozen food has fallen considerably as the supply of electricity to Brazil is being interrupted on a nightly basis and people are not using their freezers. The charity team event is over and while your team came second out of 30, such glory is short lived and the team has been disbanded back into their day jobs. You have been told by the management team that you have a week in which to define and justify a role for yourself in the company or you will be made redundant on the back of the Brazilian downturn. What do you do?

There are a number of ways of looking at this – firstly, is the redundancy package a good enough deal to allow you the opportunity of doing something else, such as further study or travel? You could take some time out using the redundancy deal as your security. Hence it could be that the worst-case scenario – redundancy – could actually be a real bonus in itself.

Secondly, you could look at other alternative employment opportunities. You have unique experience of Brazil within the retail food sector – how much would someone else like to employ you? Maybe you should send your CV to some agencies.

Thirdly, you could make a strong case to stay, based on the previous Brazil success, making the case that you could do the same elsewhere. It is not, after all, your fault that Brazil's electricity supply has become unstable! You had established a thriving market before this turn of events after a three month project here and a month over there – that's a relatively small investment for a successful national launch. Maybe the organisation would like you to look at another market?

Fourthly, you could focus on your skills and draw up the ideal job description for someone with your profile and make the case for how this could contribute to the organisation in the future.

This is actually a marvellous opportunity for you to carve out a niche for yourself within the company, or find your perfect job elsewhere. Do not look at this as a negative.

6 WHY PEOPLE FAIL EXAMS

This chapter focuses on why people fail exams, looking at the most common causes of failure. By understanding how people fail exams, you can prepare yourself so that you don't make these mistakes and hence do better than you might have done otherwise.

This chapter will cover:

- The most common reasons that people fail exams
- How different exam questions require different answers
- How to manage your time in an exam

USING THIS CHAPTER

INTRODUCTION

I was never good at passing exams. The more exams I sat, the worse I did, and this then became a downward spiral so that even the thought of an exam depressed me. Once I started marking exam scripts, I suddenly realised why I hadn't been any good at them. A lot of it is actually technique. These next few chapters focus on developing your technique to pass exams in particular, with this chapter looking specifically at why people fail exams, drawing out the learning that I've gained from marking exam scripts over the years.

FAILURE POINT 1 – NOT ANSWERING THE QUESTION SET

This can be particularly heartbreaking for markers as often you are marking the script of someone who clearly has learnt their stuff, and clearly understands the material, but unfortunately has written about something which is not the focus of the question. Some students pick up on key words in the question and then write everything they know about those key ideas but don't actually answer the question that has been asked.

If a question asks you 'compare and contrast' it is not enough simply to write everything you know about one element and ignore the other. You need to write about both elements, drawing out the similarities (comparison) and the differences (contrast). Then you need to conclude as to how similar or different the two elements are. So, for example, if you had the title 'Compare and contrast Human Resource Management with Personnel Management' you would need to argue the extent to which the two are the same, and the extent to which the two are not the same, making direct comparisons on certain criteria.

If a question asks you to 'evaluate' or 'critically evaluate' then again, simply describing something is not enough. You are being asked to make a judgement about something's value. So, for example, if you had the question 'Critically evaluate the role of women in Shakespeare's plays' you would need to examine the role of women in a number of plays, preferably offering a selection which gives variety to the role of women, and make some evaluation of this, perhaps in comparison to the role of men, or in terms of power relationships, their role within the family, their role in society, their role as 'victims', or any other ideas you have. If you are critically evaluating then you want to offer some explanation as to why this might be, which could be based on literary theory or interpretation, on history, on a contextual analysis, feminist analysis or some other basis. The choices are yours, but you do have to 'evaluate' and it does need to be about the 'role of women' specifically in 'Shakespeare's plays'. You may find a comparison with, for example, the role of women in other literature of the era, but this should be one paragraph. Do not write an essay on the role of women in literature in the sixteenth/seventeenth century – write about Shakespeare.

If a question asks you to 'discuss' then you need to have a discussion about something, thinking about every angle and concluding as to a number of points that you feel are important, whether you agree with them or not. Discussion questions often centre around a quotation. For example, if you had the question ' "Money is the root of all evil". Discuss' you would be able to talk about interpretations of evil, how money might be considered with regard to these definitions, whether it is money per se or the effect that money has on people that is the issue, and so forth. Discussion questions are the most open in terms of how wide you can trawl for ideas to put into an answer while staying on the target of answering the question. There is also a need here for you to answer the question in the discipline that you are studying. With this question, for example, a theologian might look at the concept of evil in different religions and the impact of money on each particular interpretation; a sociologist might look at the societal well-being and ill-being as an interpretation of evil, and the impact of economic prosperity on society; a geographer might look at the developing nations and the impact of external funding on the progression, or otherwise, of democracy; and so forth.

Finally, if the question asks you for a certain number of responses, make sure you include that number of responses. For example, if you have a question such as 'The early years of 0–3 are the most important in the developmental process of a child. Discuss this statement from the perspective of three different educational theorists' then you need to give three different views underpinned by three different strands of theory. Simply discussing one interpretation is not going to gain you a pass. Two might scrape you a pass, but three is what is asked for so three is what should be presented. Equally, don't waste time looking at four or five, because three is what is required.

FAILURE POINT 2 – SPENDING TOO LONG ON THE SAME POINT

The second reason that people fail exams is they spend most of the time writing about the same point. Once you have made a point, you have made it. Move on and say something else. Spending all your time on one point will only get you one mark.

Sadly, this is often when students feel they have done well when they haven't, because they come out thinking they wrote a lot because they knew a lot about the topic. This may well be true, but it does not meet the marking criteria for exams. It doesn't matter how many examples you give of the same thing, you won't get any extra marks unless the question specifically asks for lots of examples.

It is very frustrating as a marker of exam scripts to read a paper that does this as you really want the student to pass but there isn't enough there to allow them to do so, and it is not because what they have written is wrong, it is just that they haven't written enough in terms of content. Too much quantity and not enough content will not lead to a pass. One page or six pages on the same thing will not alter the mark. Don't waste your time writing too much. Be succinct and move on.

FAILURE POINT 3 – NOT KNOWING YOUR STUFF

There is an assumption in points 1 and 2 above that you have actually learnt your subject area to start off with. It doesn't matter how good you are at using your imagination, or how creative you are, if you don't know the base knowledge of your subject area, you are not going to pass your exams.

There is a difference here between not having a good memory and not having done the work. In Chapter 9 there is guidance on how to access your memory to recall what you know in the actual exam itself so that you don't 'forget' everything that you know. This is technique. You can recover from your mind going blank when you first look at the exam paper. You cannot recover, however, from your mind going blank because it is blank – i.e. you don't know what you're supposed to know in order to pass the exam.

There really is little excuse for this. Most lecturers drop very large hints as to the areas that will be covered in the exams, or you can work it out from past question papers, or from looking at the syllabus and seeing what has been covered in the assignments, and hence what has been left for the exam. Universities do not assess the same thing twice. Hence the topic area of your assignment is unlikely also to be an exam question. Learn the areas of the syllabus that have not yet been assessed as these will be the exam areas. Techniques and strategies for doing this are covered in Chapter 8 where we look at how to revise for exams.

FAILURE POINT 4 – MUDDLING CONCEPTS

Some people fail exams because they get themselves into too much of a panic in the exam hall and try to write down everything at once. This leads to an exam script which is very muddled and difficult for the marker to understand. Concepts become muddled up and the marker is left making the judgement that the student doesn't really know what they are talking about. Hence they fail.

This is most often seen when students write very long sentences. They start a sentence on one subject, and then change topic part way through the sentence, making some link in their brain that they haven't shared with the reader, and then move on again to another point. One way to avoid this is to write in short sentences to make sure that you say something and that is it. Adding the word 'and' before another point altogether is not as effective as a full stop and another sentence about another point.

Good use of English grammar can help add to the clarity of your writing on the exam paper and lead to a better mark overall. If the grammar is poor, the writing can be misinterpreted or lack the clarity necessary for it to even make sense.

If two concepts are muddled up in a paper, the marker will think that you don't understand either concept. Hence you end up losing marks that you would have gained if you'd only had time to write about one of the concepts. Clarity is important. As a marker, you really appreciate a well structured answer – it is easier to mark.

FAILURE POINT 5 – BAD EXAMPLES

Another way of raising doubt in the marker's mind as to whether or not you really do understand something is to use a bad example. If you have tried to explain something and the marker is left a little unsure as to what you mean, and then you back this up with a good example, the marker will see exactly what you mean. If however you back this up with a bad example, the marker will be convinced that you don't understand what you are talking about after all.

Choice of examples in exams is important. Make sure that they do actually illustrate the point you are trying to make, and that they are appropriate to the subject matter you are discussing. For example, if you are talking about fifteenth-century history and the role of the King, don't use an example from the eighteenth century to illustrate a point, even if it is a good example of a King behaving badly – it isn't from the fifteenth century and hence will suggest to the marker that you don't know your history at all.

For a marker, bad examples are difficult because you can never be sure if the student does know their stuff or not. The problem is that the student hasn't demonstrated their knowledge and hence it is difficult to recover marks for a student that has picked bad examples. On a lighter note, bad examples are usually the source of light relief for markers as they can be incredibly funny juxtapositions in exam scripts and are the stories shared when markers get together to moderate. My colleagues and I still remember the student that wrote about 'the role of Green Peas at the Spar' (the Spar is a local supermarket in Yorkshire) when they probably were referring to the role of Green Peace in the sinking of the Brent Spa oil platform. Sadly for that student, not only was the example flawed but the exam script overall did not amount to much and they failed, but they did give us a laugh.

The message for you here is that you don't want to provide us with jokes and light entertainment; you want to pass your exams. Don't try to amuse us – it doesn't help you pass.

FAILURE POINT 6 – RAMBLING OFF ON TANGENTS

This point links the point of muddling concepts, writing too much on the same point and not answering the question set. Sometimes students start off on one point and then get into the line of the argument so much that they start to head off at a tangent, and can actually end up writing an essay about something that isn't what the question was asking.

For markers, this is very frustrating as it is another occasion where you really want to pass a student but you can't. This happens when a student loses focus as they are writing their answer and as a marker you can see how the student's brain has gone off in another direction taking them into an area that isn't relevant. Then the rest of the essay seems to build from that.

Techniques to prevent this from occurring are provided in Chapter 9 as this type of failure is completely avoidable.

FAILURE POINT 7 – NOT DOING WHAT IS REQUIRED

Most examinations require you to answer more than one question in the time allowed. Typically you might have three essay questions in a two hour exam, allowing 40 minutes per question. Some exams allow an hour per question, some even longer. It really doesn't matter how long you have, the important point is that you spread the time evenly across all the questions that you need to answer.

If there are three essays to be answered in a paper, then the marks will be divided across the three essays. Hence the maximum score for any one essay will be 33.3 per cent. To get a first class degree, you normally need to score over 70 per cent which equates to 23.3 per cent out of 33.3 per cent. It doesn't matter how well you answer one of the questions, you still cannot score more than 33.3 per cent, so even if you score 100 per cent in that question, it will still only be 33.3 per cent overall.

If you only answer one question rather than three, you are going to fail – as the pass mark is usually 40 per cent or on some courses it is 50 per cent. Even if you answer your one question perfectly, you will still fall short of the pass mark.

If you only answer two questions rather than three, then you need to score a minimum of 40 per cent out of the possible 66.6 per cent available, or 20 per cent out of 33.3 per cent per question – which is borderline first class on two questions. This is doable, but not advisable as it is very high risk and still only achieves a pass overall. If you are capable of writing two first class essays, you should be capable of three first class essays.

If you attempt all three essays as required, you only need to score 13.3 per cent out of the 33.3 per cent in order to pass the exam overall, and everything over that is increasing your grade.

The mathematics are simple on this. It is very difficult to pass if you don't attempt the number of questions required. It is impossible to do well if you don't attempt the number of questions required. Hence make sure you check what you are required to do in the exam in terms of the number of questions to answer, and make sure you at least attempt to answer that number of questions.

FAILURE POINT 8 – BAD TIMING

Allied to the above point is timing. If you have to answer three questions then split the time for the exam into three and make sure you move on at that point in time. If you finish another question early you can always go back and add to a previous question. What you cannot do is add extra time to the end of the exam to make a better job of the last question.

Given that the marks are spread evenly across questions (unless your paper specifically tells you otherwise), it makes sense to spread the time allowed across the questions evenly.

It is very disappointing as a marker if you are marking a good script for the first essay, a pretty good second essay and then you see that the student has run out of time on the third essay and literally gives you a plan or a couple of hurried paragraphs which fail. While the student will obviously get something for this last effort, it is unlikely to be a pass and hence will pull the average for the other two essays down.

The law of diminishing returns also applies here. It is easier to pick up marks starting a new essay than it is trying to add minor points to an earlier essay. Once you have written the main bulk of the essay you will have made most of your points and scored most of your marks. Adding extra paragraphs to make minor additions is unlikely to add say another 10 per cent to your score but could take a considerable amount of time. Spending that time starting a new essay is likely to get you more than 10 per cent on that new essay as you will be able to put down lots of new ideas quite quickly.

The law of diminishing returns basically means that the extra marks gained goes down the longer you spend on an essay, and hence it is better to move on and leave an essay unfinished than finish an essay and not leave enough time for the next.

FAILURE POINT 9 – LACK OF COHESIVENESS

Most exams include the requirement to write essays; indeed many exams only require essays. An essay is a length of writing that argues a point. It has a start, a middle, and an end. Chapter 11 looks at assessments generally and covers how to write a good essay, but for the purpose of an exam, you are looking at writing a short piece that answers the question by linking the points you make into a cohesive argument.

Another reason students fail exams is that their answers lack this cohesiveness. Some students panic and literally give you a brain dump of everything they know about a subject, in no particular order. This also usually fails to answer the question set, but more importantly, it doesn't actually make sense.

As a marker, this is another of those frustrating scripts to read as you generally feel that the student does know something about what they are being asked, but they haven't expressed it in a way that allows you as a marker to ascertain what it is that they know. As a result, the student is likely to fail.

FAILURE POINT 10 – UNREADABLE WRITING

This may sound obvious, but if the marker cannot read your writing, you are not going to pass! It is almost a peculiar anomaly that you are required to handwrite examinations as virtually everything else you will do in your life will require you to type on a keyboard rather than write on a page. As computers have become more pervasive in our lives, we practise our handwriting less, and most people's handwriting – like any skill – deteriorates with lack of practice. We get slower at writing neatly, and for many of us the 'neatly' bit also disappears. When you then find yourself in an exam, you are expected to write neatly and quickly, and for 2–3 hours non-stop.

Again, some techniques to help with this are discussed in Chapter 9, but it is important that you practise speed writing in advance of the exams to ensure that your script is readable. Nobody has ever passed an exam when a marker cannot read their script – and you will not be given the opportunity to come in and read it to someone, or to rewrite it more neatly.

WORKED EXAMPLE

This example has been adapted from an examination in English, in which the candidates were asked to 'Explain the ideas that are suggested in the extract from *Jurassic Park*', a book that was written by an author named Michael Crichton. Crichton's books are always a combination of a good adventure story and some scientific theory, such that the adventure explores the scientific theory. In *Jurassic Park*, the scientific theory that is being explored is that of Chaos Theory. Names have been replaced with character descriptors to help you make sense of the answers.

The first example scored around 30 per cent; the second scored around 55 per cent and the final example scored 80 per cent. Each is presented and then discussed in turn.

Example 1

The ideas suggested in the extract is that the scientist thinks park owner is mad. He has built a dinosaur theme park and recreated dinosaurs 'because he can'. This means he has the money and can buy the expertise to do this and hence he can do what he wants.

The park owner is so concerned with money, and the millions that the park will make for him once it opens that scientist labels him 'mad'. He does come over as rather mad as he is a larger than life character and is very generous in the way he is entertaining his guests. Such generosity can be seen as mad.

The extract questions the right of one person to recreate the life of a species that has become extinct. The park owner is likened to playing God by giving life to a species that no longer exists – the dinosaurs. Just because they can create the dinosaurs does not mean that they should create the dinosaurs, is the argument, and how are they going to control them. This will be done by the mechanisms and fencing that has been designed for the park and is the central theme of the book. The dinosaurs are kept like they are in a big zoo, but in cages big enough to give them some freedom. In terms of the design of the park there does not seem to be much that hasn't been thought of and hence it doesn't seem mad at all.

The argument is about how a strong willed, old man wants to spend his money towards the end of his life, and the legacy that he wants to leave behind for his grandchildren. He wants to do something different so that they have something to remember him by.

Why did this script fail?

Firstly, the marker made a note that 'a stronger focus on the requirements of the question would assist this response'. The students were asked to 'explain the ideas that are suggested in the extract'. The marker felt that the answer demonstrated a very limited understanding of the passage but was rather descriptive in terms of it being about a mad old man creating a theme park because he was rich. The marker also felt the student appeared more interested in arguing a case for the right of rich people to spend their money how they want than explaining the ideas presented in the passage.

In terms of the points outlined in this chapter, then, the student fell at the first hurdle in that they didn't do what was asked of them in the question; secondly they went on for too long making the same point, and thirdly didn't really know their stuff. They also rambled off on a tangent (money) and the presentation is poor both in terms of cohesiveness and use of English.

Reading this script, you don't feel confident that the student knows what they are talking about, or really understands the issues. That is the reason that this script failed.

Example 2

Jurassic Park by Michael Crichton, is a work of fiction that explores the application of chaos theory to a prehistoric theme park. The extract outlines the chaos theorist's and other scientists objections to the development of the theme park, by exploring how chaos theory means that they will never be able to control the on-going effects of what they have done.

Chaos theory is the idea that you cannot be certain of the effects that any single action will have. The traditional example is that a butterfly flapping its wings in Hawaii can cause a hurricane in China. The power of chaos theory is that the effects of an action are on-going and have further ramifications beyond those anticipated. This is not understood by the theme park owner who simply sees the issue in economic terms.

The passage illustrates how money can corrupt the brain. It shows how money can power and give one person power over another. The scientists have all the knowledge and yet are powerless to do anything because they don't have the money. Hence the mad theme park owner is in control, and is setting the boundaries and rules governing the scientists as if they are prisoners.

This could leave the scientists feeling alienated. They are not allowed to leave the theme park. It is like they are being held prisoners which will make them isolated and lonely and they may also become mad like the theme park owner. They are also likely to become deskilled from their alienation and isolation.

People who are held as prisoners often have high mental degradation. The text Jurassic Park explores issues around mental degradation from money, science and isolation. Some of these issues are explained better than others in the text.

Why did this script not get a first?

Firstly, the script starts better than it ends. The beginning is an objective overview of the script, telling the reader that they understand the context of the passage and the fact that it is fiction within a scientific context. The script is well-structured and presents a coherent argument. Unfortunately, the script falls off towards the end with sweeping generalisations and a shift away from the content of the extract to wider interpretations of the book, which are largely unsubstantiated. Finally, the interpretation offered has gone to an extreme beyond that suggested in the text and hence has taken a tangent that favours the author rather than a line that is evidenced in the text, or indeed in the book itself.

This script is a good illustration of how a student can start well with an answer and then go downhill, but it also shows that a good start is good enough to get you a clear pass mark.

Example 3

Jurassic Park by Michael Crichton deals with the way in which decisions are made in society without real consideration of the knock-on effects and consequences. This is explored through the introduction of a range of scientists to the story, in particular a chaos theorist, a palaeontologist and an expert in dinosaurs.

The lack of consideration of chaos theory is explored through the re-creation of dinosaurs on a theme park island. The moral and ethical issue of whether or not this should have been achieved is explored in the extract with the chaos theorist pointing that just because they could, doesn't mean that they should. This raises the ethical questions about who has the right to create life, or even re-create life after a species has become extinct through the development of nature. This could be linked to Darwinian theories of survival of the fittest.

The moral element is only one dimensions. Another is that of chaos theory and the fact that we cannot control for all the consequences of our actions. The best known example that is used to describe chaos theory is that of a butterfly flapping its wings in one part of the world and causing a hurricane in another part of the world, because the motion of the wing flapping causes a change in the air current that has a greater effect on wind patterns, and so forth until you get your hurricane in another part of the world.

In this extract, the chaos theorist is arguing that recreating the dinosaurs was not a good idea because it has upset nature and nobody knows what the consequences of such an upset will be. For example, they re-grew plants that had died out with the dinosaurs, and these may pollinate in such a way that the wind carries their seeds off the island and they take root on the mainland, which in turn means other plant life is killed as these plants take over, and then birds and insects die because these plants are poisonous to them, and so forth.

In conclusion, the ideas expressed in the extract suggest that a person is mad to think that they can control nature, because the laws of nature and chaos theory will mean that nature cannot be controlled and hence we will not be able to control the consequences of the creation of the prehistoric theme park.

Why did this script get a first class mark?

The marker felt the student had demonstrated a clear understanding of the ideas being conveyed in the passage, particularly the broader explanation of the underpinning theory and links to other theoretical ideas. Examples used are appropriate and illustrate the point being made, and there is a good contrast of the local discussion re the creation of dinosaurs on the island and then the wider implications re nature in general. Even given all of this, the answer would have scored even more highly if the student had acknowledged the fact that the passage was fiction set within a scientific context as this adds to the weight of the text, and if the theoretical ideas had been referenced/acknowledged more fully to authors writing in the field.

CHAPTER SUMMARY

This chapter clearly outlines the mistakes that are commonly made by students that lead to them failing their examinations. These are not the only reasons that people fail, but the most common, and all of them can be redressed through technique, practice and further development of skills. If you can recognise yourself within this chapter, then that is very positive as the rest of this book will help you succeed. If you don't see your own work within this chapter and are still failing, then you might want to talk to your tutors to see if they can help you identify what you are doing wrong. Once you realise what you are doing wrong, you can do something to address the problem. You are not failing exams because you are stupid – you are failing because you have got some part of the studying or examination technique wrong.

BUSINESS GAME

Your pitch to your organisation to launch in another country was successful and the country you were allocated was Kenya. Unfortunately, the Kenyan market proved to be very different to the Brazilian market, so although you applied the same techniques in writing your report, the findings were very different. You argued to the company that the market was not ready for your products and there was no point in your going out there at that time. The company is unhappy at this result and again your job is on the line. You have been asked to present yourself to the MD for a discussion about your future in the organisation. How can you prepare for the discussion?

The key point here is going to be about how you have actually saved the organisation money rather than wasted it. If you hadn't been so thorough, rigorous and disciplined about your approach to your research, you would have come up with a false picture and the organisation would have invested a lot of money launching into a market that was not ready for them. Hence your application of technique, knowledge and skill has led to a success and not a failure in terms of the company's future. You could focus on how companies make mistakes launching into the wrong markets, and how your techniques have avoided that.

7 ▶ PREPARING FOR EXAMINATIONS

This chapter focuses on the preparation that needs to take place prior to you going into the examination hall to sit your exams. It covers both your physical preparation in terms of diet and sleep habits, and your mental preparation in terms of positive thinking and motivation.

This chapter will cover:

- How to be motivated about sitting an exam
- What to take with you to the examination itself
- How to best prepare yourself physically for sitting an exam

USING THIS CHAPTER

INTRODUCTION

This chapter focuses on what you do in that period of time before an examination, without specifically looking at revision of the work involved – that is in the next chapter. Being prepared for an examination is not all about revision – although revision is an essential element – but there is the mental preparation, physical preparation, and finding a routine that works for you. This chapter helps you understand why you feel the way you do when you walk into an examination, and offers advice on how to improve that feeling so that you are better prepared for success than failure.

LESSON FROM THE OLYMPICS 2008

The British sports team at the 2008 Olympics performed better than any other UK team has performed at an Olympic games, breaking more records and winning more medals than has previously been achieved. Much of this success has been attributed to the lottery funding as it has not only allowed the athletes to focus on their training rather than earning a living, but it has also funded a range of support services such as psychologists, nutritionists, and so forth.

The sports psychologists, in particular, seem to have made an impact on the rowing team. Previous rowing multiple gold medallist Matthew Pinsent was commentating at the 2008 games and talked a lot about the hour before you get on to the water to start the race, and how crucial that was in your preparation as maintaining focus while keeping the nerves under control was vital to how you perform.

The nutritionists were mentioned by some of the winning cyclists in their post-event interviews, highlighting the difference that the right food being consumed at the right time was making to their performance. Indeed, the British cycling team had literally taken their routine to pieces and put it back together after it had been scrutinised by experts, making changes to their equipment, their costumes, their diets and their routines. The result was more gold medals in the cycling events than has ever been achieved before, to the point that Britain dominated the cycling across the board.

So why draw this out now? The point is that going into an exam is much like preparing for an Olympic event. You want to perform your best. You're going to be judged by someone else. You're in a competition in that you want to score most highly against the criteria. In short, you want to win.

THE NIGHT BEFORE THE EXAM

The one thing that all the athletes said prior to completing their events was that they were going to go back to the village, relax, eat and get an early night for the next day. This may sound simple and obvious, but there was a discipline with which every athlete said it. 'Relax, eat and get an early night'.

Staying up all night trying to cram in last minute revision is not going to help you pass your exams; indeed it is likely to hinder the process. A tired mind does not do well in exams, so it is important to get a good night's sleep before an exam. This is also aided by refraining from alcohol and not consuming too much caffeine.

NUTRITIONAL CONTRIBUTION

Try to eat something relatively plain, filling, but not heavy. Pasta is usually a good meal before an exam, rather than a curry or Chinese. Pizza can be quite heavy and hard to digest. You don't want to risk having an upset stomach the next day, or having indigestion during the night. Eat something that is easy to digest but fills you up.

In the morning, eat a good breakfast. It is very hard to concentrate if you are hungry. Don't have too much caffeine as this will set your mind buzzing, and don't have too much sugar either as this will raise your blood sugar levels to a high which is likely to drop to a low during the exam.

Take some food into the exam with you (if you are allowed) in case you get hungry or suffer from a drop in blood sugar. A bar of chocolate or other snack of this sort is usually best as you can get an instant boost from consuming it part-way through if you need it. In consideration to the other candidates, try to get something that is quiet to unwrap and eat.

Don't drink more caffeine than you would normally drink as this will alter your levels of concentration from your normal performance. A caffeine buzz is unlikely to help you pass and is more likely to contribute to poorer performance.

Take a bottle of water into the exam with you (if you are allowed) as you are likely to get a bit thirsty or dry-mouthed during the period of the exam. Two or three hours is a long time to go without a drink when you are in a fairly dry, concentrated atmosphere.

THE RIGHT EQUIPMENT

Most of the time that you are a student you will work on your computer. You may even be a very fast typist by now, and all your assignments will have been typed. Handwriting is something that you scribble down as notes on handouts, or write the odd note or list in. Handwriting is not a skill you will practise much, other than in exams.

It is important, therefore, that you have the correct writing equipment for your exam. This may sound silly, as a pen is a pen, but this is not the case. Some pens are thicker than others, some are rounder, others are hexagonal. Some people like to hold a thicker pen, others a thinner pen. Some people prefer to write with a ball-point, others with a rollerball.

Find a pen that you are happy to write with for a couple of hours. It is highly likely that you will get cramp in your hand or arm during your exam, but this can be minimised by experimenting with different types of pens.

If you find yourself writing with a pen you don't like, it is irritating and distracts your mind from thinking about the answers. It can also be harder work physically if the ink doesn't flow well from the pen, or if the nib catches on the paper because it has a rough edge. These little things are all things you want to find out before you go into the examination hall, not during the first half hour of the exam itself.

WEARING THE RIGHT CLOTHES

Again, this might sound simple and obvious, but it is important to think about what you are going to wear for your exams. Firstly, you don't want to wear anything that will be too tight as this will get uncomfortable when you are sitting down for a couple of hours.

Secondly, you want to wear something which is loose around the arms and shoulders so that you have ease of movement to write.

Thirdly, wear layers. Sometimes exam halls get too hot with all the people that are in them so you might want to take off a layer as the exam progresses and you find yourself getting too hot. Alternatively, the hall might be colder than you expected and you might want to add a layer of clothing to keep yourself warm.

Clothing may sound like an irrelevancy, but if you are wearing the wrong clothes and are uncomfortable then it will distract you from the task at hand of writing the best paper you can. Choose your wardrobe the night before and leave your clothes out for the morning.

Finally, for those of you who wear jewellery – think about taking it off for the exam.

Bracelets will clatter on the writing table which is a distraction not just to yourself but to others; the same thing can happen with pendants on chains round your neck as you are likely to lean forwards more when writing an exam script than you would normally during an average day. Rings can interfere with how you hold the pen, getting sweaty and causing loss of grip as the exam progresses. Rather than worrying about taking them off during the exam, take them off before you leave home.

BEFORE YOU LEAVE THE HOUSE

Have a plan of what you will take into the examination hall with you and tick it off the list when you pack it into your bag on the morning of the exam. Take a spare of everything in case a friend has forgotten something and wants to borrow it, or you get extra hungry or thirsty. Have everything packed the night before the first exam so that you are not in a panic in the morning, and then refresh the bag before each subsequent exam.

Your list might look something like this:

Item	Quantity	Packed
Bottle of water	2	√
Chocolate bar	2	
Pens	6	
Calculator (if necessary)	2	
Notes (if allowed in an open book exam)		
Watch	1	
Desk clock	1	

So, in comparison to the Olympic cyclists, we have now looked at your equipment, your costume, your nutrition, and your routine. The final element that led to Olympic success was the sports psychologists, so let's turn now to look at the mental preparation that you need to undertake when preparing for your exams.

THE IMPORTANCE OF SELF-BELIEF

People's beliefs about their personal capabilities influence what they try to accomplish, and how they respond to successes and setbacks on the way. It is unlikely that the rowers at the Olympics would win the gold medal if they didn't really believe that they could. In fact, they probably wouldn't even have entered the Olympics as they wouldn't think themselves good enough to try. Look at some of the younger athletes who went. They all went saying they were 'there to get the experience' because evidently some research has shown that athletes perform better at their second Olympics rather than their first. None of these young Olympians are winning and one can't help wondering if they would be getting Bronze medals perhaps if they went with the belief that they could win.

Self-efficacy is a study of those factors that people can control, and hence it is the study of human potential and possibilities, not limitations. Bandura's original definition of self-efficacy is 'the conviction that one can successfully execute the behaviour required to produce particular outcomes' (1977: 193). Later, he focused more on skills, adding that 'self-efficacy is concerned with generative capabilities, not with component acts' (Bandura, 1986: 397). The basic idea is that the more you believe you can do something, the more likely you are to attempt it, and the more likely you are to learn and master the skills that allow you to succeed. Hence a positive spiral of belief leading to skill, leading to performance is enacted.

If you walk into an examination thinking you are going to fail it, then you are more likely to do so than if you walk in believing that you can pass it. This is not simply about being confident. You can be confident and arrogant and fail. It is about having the requisite belief in your skill and knowledge to help you succeed rather than succumbing to self-doubt.

One reason that strong self-efficacy can lead to success is that it leads to effective self-regulation and persistence. People who believe in their ability to achieve work hard to attain that achievement. They set themselves goals and are disciplined in their approach to achieving them. This takes us back to Chapter 2 which raised the issues of self-discipline when studying, and the development of rigour.

THE IMPORTANCE OF CONTEXT

Self-efficacy is also influenced by situation and context. If you do not have the right environment in which to develop your capability, then your capability will be limited. Your environment should sit well with your goals, so if your goals at a particular point in time are to read four articles, then the environment should be one that you find conducive to reading. This is likely to be a quiet space with a comfortable chair and space for your laptop. It is unlikely to be a coffee shop or social area. Equally the environment must be warm enough, light enough, and safe enough for you to achieve your goals. You need to have the right equipment in your environment otherwise it is difficult to achieve the goal, if not impossible, and it helps if the environment is supportive rather than hostile. If all these environmental factors feel right, then you are likely to feel that you are in control and hence can focus on the task at hand and achieve your goal. If the environmental factors are wrong, you are likely to focus on improving the environment rather than achieving the goal required.

MANAGING STRESS

There are a number of elements of exams that people get stressed about:

- The limited time factor, i.e. you have to answer a set number of questions in a set time
- The unknown, i.e. you don't know what the questions are
- The fear of failure, i.e. you don't want to do badly
- The fear of forgetting, i.e. you worry that you are going to forget everything you know
- The fear of not knowing, i.e. you worry that you are not going to know the answers to the question
- The rigid regime, i.e. you can't communicate with others or move around the room
- ... and so forth

There are two main sources of stress that are underpinning these: first is the feeling of being powerless, and second is the need for approval.

Feeling powerless is a major cause of stress throughout our lives, not just at exam time. If we get stuck in a traffic jam we are powerless – and what do we do? We look at our watches to remind ourselves of just how powerless we are by watching time tick by without being able to do anything about it. The way to regain power is to take ownership of the problem. In earlier chapters the concept of the locus of control came up – whether we take responsibility for our own lives or whether life happens to us. A similar concept applies here. The way to regain power is to take back the control by taking ownership of the problem. Powerful people own their own problems.

This is a key point to remember whenever you are feeling stressed because you feel powerless. Powerful people own their own problems. Hence the way to regain power when you are feeling powerless is to redefine the problem so that you own it. For example, you might feel powerless because you are not allowed to move around and communicate in an exam. This can redefined to 'I feel stressed because I can't move around or communicate during an exam'. Now you can do something about this. You can stop feeling stressed about it. You can't change the fact that you can't move around or communicate, but you can change feeling stressed about it. So, you might be thinking, how do you stop feeling stressed about it?

Acknowledging the fact that you are allowing yourself to feel stressed about something you can do nothing about is a good starting point. Once you recognise what the problem is, you can do something about it. Stopping feeling stressed about something takes discipline and practice, but basically you have to keep telling yourself that you are not going to allow yourself to be stressed by it; it is a waste of energy and emotion. This does take practice.

Driving is a good place to practise this. The next time you are in a traffic queue, look around you. Everyone will be getting angry; their expressions will become tense; they'll be as close as possible to the car in front of them; and then, if someone wants to pull in from a slip road, they speed up as much as possible to get even closer to the car in front so that there is no way that person is getting in in front of them. What are people doing? They are driving around highly stressed when they can't do anything about it. Try a different tactic. Tell yourself you are not going to be stressed – you are going to use the time as thinking time and think of it as a gift. Now watching other drivers becomes a source of amusement. How cross are they? And how easy is it to get them even crosser? For example, slow down and signal out not one but two cars from the filter lane that is trying to join your lane and watch how angry the person behind you gets. Also, think what a good impression you've made on the two drivers you've let in, and how you have improved their day, and all for what – a 2 second addition to your queuing time.

The ability to stay calm by reframing what is causing you stress is an exceedingly powerful skill to learn, not just for exams, but for life generally. It not only gives you a very strong internal locus of control (Heider, 1958), but it gives you power by not draining your energy and emotions and allowing you to stay focused.

List six things that cause you stress about exams. For each try to reframe it in such a way that you can take ownership. Finally outline what action you will take to reduce or remove the stress.

Cause of stress	Reframe to regain power	Solution

Seeking approval is another main cause of stress that underpins a lot of exam anxiety. Fear of failure is based upon seeking approval. If we fail other people will not approve – our parents, our tutors, our friends, even ourselves. Other people's approval can be such a powerful driver that we can make ourselves sick trying to achieve it. Why? What is the implication for us if they don't approve? Will we actually approve of ourselves more if we stop trying to meet the expectations of others but rather reach for our own goals?

If you are studying for your degree for someone other than yourself, the fear of failure will be multiplied, and the stress of sitting the exams will be even greater. You should be doing your degree for yourself; it is for your future. It is very difficult to remain motivated to study for a degree that you do not want to be doing. Think about what is motivating you and how this motivation might be causing you stress.

SOURCES OF MOTIVATION

Ford (1992) outlines how motivational systems theory principles can be used for motivating humans. These can be applied directly to individuals in exam situations, and may help you realise what it is that is blocking your success in exams – it may be linked to your motivation. Table 7.1 is adapted from Ford (1992: 220) where he outlines 17 principles of motivational systems theory and what their core idea is. A final column has been added to put these in the context of your sitting your exams.

Table 7.1 **Motivational systems theory principles**

Motivational systems theory principle	Core idea	Reframe with regard to examinations
The principle of unitary functioning	One always deals with a whole person-in-context	You are more than simply an exam candidate, you are a person who is currently a student sitting examinations
The motivational triumvirate principle	Goals, emotions and personal agency beliefs must all be influenced to facilitate motivation	In order to be motivated to pass your exams you need to want to achieve a good degree, want to do well this time round, and feel that you are in control of your success or failure
The responsive environment principle	Relationships are as important as techniques	In order to do well you need the support of those around you as well as techniques in how to pass
The principle of goal activation	Little else matters if there is no relevant goal in place	The exams don't matter if you are not ambitious about your degree or what it enables you to do in the longer term
The principle of goal salience	Goals must be clear and compelling to transform concerns into intentions	Be clear about what you want to achieve and why

$\rightarrow$

Table 7.1 continued

Motivational systems theory principle	Core idea	Reframe with regard to examinations
The multiple goals principle	Multiple goals can strengthen motivation substantially	Getting a good degree is just the start; have ambitions for what that will allow you to do beyond university
The principle of goal alignment	Multiple goals must be aligned rather than in conflict to enhance motivation	Make sure your goals don't conflict; getting a first and having a great social life, for example, might conflict
The feedback principle	Goals lose their potency in the absence of clear and informative feedback	Read/listen to the feedback tutors give you; it will keep you on track
The flexible standards principle	Flexible standards protect against demotivation and facilitate self-improvement	If you suffer a failure, don't view it as irrecoverable, but more as an opportunity to learn for next time
The optimal challenge principle	Challenging but attainable standards enhance motivation	Keep your goals realistic; setting milestones on the way can help so that you can see that are you on target as you progress through your studies
The principle of direct evidence	Clear, specific evidence is needed to influence capability and context beliefs	Check on your marks and progress regularly to reassure yourself that you can do this
The reality principle	Personal agency beliefs ultimately require real skills and a truly responsive environment	If you are feeling powerless, reframe the issue so that you take control and place yourself in an environment where you can do that
The principle of emotional activation	Strong emotions indicate and facilitate strong motivational patterns	The more you want success, the more you will work to achieve it
The 'do it' principle	If a person is capable, just try to get them started	Once you get started, you will be amazed at how much you can do
The principle of incremental versus transformational change	Incremental change is easier and safer; transform only with care and as a last resort	Don't look for huge changes; progress at a steady rate in your pursuit of your studies

Table 7.1 continued

Motivational systems theory principle	Core idea	Reframe with regard to examinations
The equifinality principle	There are many ways to motivate humans – if progress is slow, keep trying	If you have lost your motivation for any particular reason, look for another reason to underpin your ongoing success and set yourself a new set of goals
The principle of human respect	People must be treated with respect to produce enduring motivational effects	Treat your tutors with respect and they will do likewise to you; choose your workmates carefully so that everyone pulls their weight

Source: Ford (1992: 220). Reproduced with permission.

MANAGING YOUR TIME

Generally, if you manage your stress well you will manage your time well. This is because you will feel in control of what you are doing, when, where and with whom. The basic principles of time management are to use your time effectively and efficiently. That is, use your time doing those tasks which achieve the most for you (i.e. effectiveness), and achieve the most using the least amount of time (i.e. efficiency). Your time is a scarce and non-renewable resource, so once it has passed it has gone forever and cannot be regained.

It can be quite a useful exercise to review your week to see how effective and efficient you have been. This also allows you to set your objectives for the next week and so forth. Think about your week and what you were trying to achieve. Note down your objectives, whether or not you achieved them, and how long it took you to achieve them.

Objective	Achieved (Yes/No)	Time taken to achieve/amount of effort expended

Was the amount of effort expended/time taken to achieve the objective a good use of your time? If not, what can you do differently next time to improve your use of time? Sometimes this can be a case of dropping your 'perfectionist tendencies' and doing something 'well enough' rather than 'perfectly'. For example, reading an article as outlined in Chapter 2 rather than reading an article from the first word to the last; spending your time studying and then cooking once your friends arrive rather than having a meal pre-prepared for them; and so forth.

Don't waste time on jobs that don't really need doing when you have a deadline to meet. We are all very good at doing this – it is called avoidance tactics – but it doesn't move the deadline and only hinders your overall effectiveness.

You may find that you are more effective at one end of the day than the other. Some people wake up raring to go and are highly efficient early in the morning but flag in the evenings; others find it difficult to get going in the mornings but come into their own at night. If this is you, then tackle the important tasks at the time of day that you are most effective. If you are a morning person, get up and work on your assignments and exam preparation. In the evenings you can read more widely and prepare for seminars.

One way of improving your use of time is to cut down on the number of interruptions that you get. This may mean turning off your mobile phone; logging out of e-mail; finding a quiet space to work and not telling anyone where you are going; or deliberately staying in when you know all of your friends have gone out. Interruptions are costly because they not only take up time, but they waste the time before and immediately after the interruption as you need to go back and pick up on what you were doing because you will have lost your train of thought. When you are reading this can be particularly time-consuming as you can lose the gist of the paper and need to go back and re-read it.

PREPARING FOR PRESENTATIONS

Evidently public speaking is one of the greatest fears most people hold in life. The thought of standing up in front of people and presenting to them can be terrifying. Nerves take over and the delivery is weak. This can be avoided. Even seasoned presenters get nervous before giving a presentation so don't think you are alone in your nervous state. The important point to learn is how to channel those nerves into positive energy so that they enhance rather than detract from your presentation.

As with exams, practice is important. Rehearse your presentation half a dozen times with family, friends, house-mates, anyone that will listen. Time your rehearsals so that you know your presentation lasts as long as it should.

Again, as for exams, dress appropriately. Wear something that is smart and comfortable and makes you feel like you are acting the part of the presenter. Don't go to a presentation wearing jeans and a sweater as you will feel like a 'poor student'. Go wearing your best work clothes or a suit so that you feel like a professional. Image is important here – it is a presentation.

Having the right equipment is also important. Have a set of visual aids that guide you through the order of the presentation so you don't have to remember what to say next. In addition, have a set of notes that are easy to read. Powerpoint is a great package. You can have your series of slides which guide you through the presentation, but can also print out notes which you can refer to for each slide in the event that you forget what you wanted to say.

Breathing exercises can be useful if you feel yourself reaching a panic point as you enter the room and stand up to speak. Try to slow your breathing, ensuring that you breathe in and out for the same amount of time. Try to speak slowly – most people speak too quickly when they are presenting so if you feel you are going horrendously slowly you are probably talking at about the right pace. The news is read on the television at approximately 120 words per minute which is really quite slow but it doesn't sound it. The speed of normal conversation is closer to 150 words per minute, so presentations should be slower than conversations to give the audience the chance to take in what you are saying. If you feel panic, stop talking, breathe and count to five. Then continue. Nobody will notice – it will seem like a natural pause and give you time to calm your nerves.

Finally, know your stuff. You'll be amazed at how much you do know once you start to talk about it, and look at questions being asked as an opportunity to share your knowledge and enthusiasm.

Actually that is the final point. Be enthusiastic. Enthusiasm can carry you through a lot with regard to presentations. If you are enthusiastic about your subject the audience is likely to be also. If you are bored with the subject, the audience will be also.

There is more about how to go about putting presentations together as assignments in Chapter 11. Their inclusion here is as much about showing you that preparation for exams is the same as any preparation, as the same principles apply.

PREPARING FOR LAB-WORK ASSESSMENTS

Again, the lessons are much the same in preparing for a lab-work assessment, but perhaps the emphasis varies slightly. Having the right equipment is paramount, as is the right clothes, or you might do something silly like set yourself on fire.

For lab work you need to know precisely what it is you are going to be doing (if you are allowed to know) so that you can read around the subject area and prepare yourself for any mishaps that are known to occur with that sort of work. Have some recovery strategies ready for if an experiment 'goes wrong', and make sure you have lots of recording equipment available (be it notebooks or a digital voice recorder) so that you can record exactly what you have done.

Again with lab work, if panic sets in, take five seconds out, breathe, and then continue. Five seconds is not going to matter to the time overall, but it will give you time to take stock, calm down and then get going again.

If you find your hands are shaking, try to anchor them as much as possible either by holding on to something solid, or by resting them on the workbench. This will make you feel more secure and less shaky.

Preparation is key to lab-work assessments. If you get the opportunity to practise in advance then do so – even if it means staying late in a lab on your own, you won't regret it. Know where all the equipment that you will need is kept in case something you are using breaks down or is faulty. Try to be in a position whereby you don't have to rely on lab technicians – it's great if they are there to help, but don't depend on it. You don't want your success or failure to be dependent on someone else – take responsibility for yourself.

Again, make notes in advance of what you will or may need to do. Lab work is not usually a memory test; notes are generally allowed. Lab work is about demonstrating your practical skills, so the more practised you are, the better.

PREPARING FOR AN ORAL EXAMINATION OR VIVA

Here the key to preparation is knowing your stuff. Oral examinations or vivas occur for two purposes: firstly, to allow you to defend your work such as in the case of a doctoral submission or a submission for a masters by research. This type of defence is usually only conducted in research degrees. The second type of oral examination, and that is most common in the case of undergraduate students, is basically – I hate to say it – to check that your work is your own and has not been plagiarised (copied) from elsewhere.

Examiners will be looking for a number of things in this type of oral examination: firstly, that you do actually know and understand the content of the written submission that you are being examined on; and secondly, that you can express this in language similar to that in the written submission. Now, if your work is your own, you have absolutely nothing to worry about in an oral examination. I have never known a student not be able to answer questions about their own assignment. Everything goes wrong, however, for students who have plagiarised and the oral examination is a means by which they are caught.

So, if you are called for an oral examination, try to ascertain why. Sometimes markers want to establish that a piece of work truly is first class; other times it is because they suspect it might be plagiarised. If it is the latter and you have plagiarised it just come clean with the examiners either before the examination or at the start of it. You will not be able to defend a plagiarised piece of work – the examiners will break you. Now if you are reading this and are scared that the examiners will break you when it is your piece of work – they won't. It becomes patently obvious very quickly when someone talks about their assignment as to whether or not they wrote it. It is, of course, sensible to read through the assignment again in advance of the examination, just to refresh your memory.

A final type of oral examination is that for a foreign language. Here the preparation involves keeping calm, making sure you have done any preparation required (perhaps reading a passage of text), and that you have practised speaking in the language being examined as much as possible in the lead-up to the examination. If possible, speak to native language speakers rather than other students, as their sense of flow of the language is bound to be superior.

CHAPTER SUMMARY

This chapter has hopefully drilled into you the importance of preparation for any type of examination. Even the simple details of clothes, equipment and breakfast can help calm you if they are prepared in advance. It allows you to start your examination day with simple routines that go to plan, setting the scene for success and building on achievements, rather than running round in a panic trying to find a clean pair of socks to wear, and grabbing a sugar fix with caffeine on the run. Management of stress and management of time are clearly related: manage time well and you will be less stressed; manage stress well and time will manage itself. Being well prepared for an examination makes sure that nothing detracts from your performance in the examination hall, and allows you to focus on your success.

BUSINESS GAME

Your organisation has asked you to do the keynote presentation at their internal annual conference to all 900 employees. You have got to talk for half an hour on 'internationalising the organisation'. How would you prepare for the presentation?

The obvious points to think about are the content of the presentation, how it is organised, how it is presented so it is not boring and people stay focused, and how it is presented in terms of visual aids. In addition there are the elements of where you will be presenting (check out the room), what you will wear (check the outfit still fits and is comfortable), and controlling your nerves and stress.

References

Bandura, A. (1977) Self-efficacy: Toward a unifying theory of behaviour change. *Psychological Review*, 84, 191–215.

Bandura, A. (1986) *Social Foundations of Thought and Action: A social cognitive theory.* Upper Saddle River, NJ: Prentice Hall.

Ford, M. E. (1992) *Motivating Humans.* Thousand Oaks, CA: Sage Publications.

Heider, F. (1958) *The Psychology of Interpersonal Relations.* New York: John Wiley & Sons.

8 ▶ REVISING

This chapter focuses on revision. If you get your revision strategy right then you will know all you need to know to pass the exam. If you don't, you won't. It's as simple as that. It is important to start revising early enough, and to cover a range of topic areas that are likely to come up rather than the topic areas that you like best.

This chapter will cover:

- How to choose what to revise
- Revision techniques to help you embed your learning
- Planning your revision timetable

USING THIS CHAPTER

INTRODUCTION

Some people spend hours doing what they think is 'revision' without actually learning anything. Often this is because it is not revision at all, but learning for the first time. Revision is exactly what it says: re-vision – looking at work again to embed the learning and ensure that you remember it when under the pressure of the examination situation. There are lots of different strategies that students can employ when undertaking their revision. Not every strategy works for every student, but you should be able to find out which ones work for you quite quickly. Don't try to master every strategy – stick to those that work best for you and don't worry about the ones that don't. The important strategy that everyone should do is past exam questions. This not only focuses you on revising the course content, but also gives you practice in exam technique. Developing exam technique is a key component of the revision process. You are revising to pass an exam and for no other purpose. Practising the exam therefore is the most commonsense activity you can do.

WHY REVISE?

This may sound like a stupidly obvious question, but is it? Some people revise to make sure they've learnt enough to pass their exam. They see revision as a memory test. Other people revise to embed the learning they gained through the module so that they can express this better in their exam. They see revision as a means of enhancing learning. Others revise because they think they should, because everyone else does. They see revision as a chore. So what is the point of revision?

Basically you undertake revision in order to give yourself the best possibility of demonstrating your knowledge, skill and understanding under exam conditions. Note that this is not so that you can show the examiner everything you know; nor is it about showing the examiner everything you have managed to remember; it is about demonstrating your knowledge, skill and understanding under exam conditions.

Obviously to demonstrate knowledge you will have to show that you know something, so there does have to be some knowledge of facts; understanding however is demonstrated through the development of reason and argument; and skill is demonstrated through the means by which the argument is developed, and the question is answered.

Revision is not all about remembering – that is just one part of it. It is also about developing the skill to demonstrate understanding under exam conditions. This is another reason why answering past questions is key to any revision programme.

SELECTING YOUR REVISION TOPICS

There is an argument that says you should revise the whole syllabus as you never know what might come up. This is true to a degree, but in most universities in the UK the assessment system for modules is based on a 'learning outcomes' model. Fundamental to the learning outcomes model is that the curriculum is expressed in terms of the outcomes of the student's learning on the module. Equally fundamental is the idea that each outcome needs to be assessed to ensure the student has achieved the module outcomes, and that each outcome is only assessed once.

Now not every academic is completely aware of this, and so to be on the safe side you should check with your tutors, but as a general rule, on the basis that each outcome should only be assessed once, the area in which you did your assignment (if there was one) will not be covered again in the exam.

In many ways this seems harsh since this is the area that you now know best as you've put all the effort into submitting the assignment; it does also make sense though since what is the point in asking students the same thing twice?

So, the first area you can drop is that of your assignment. How else can you narrow down the field? Have a look at past exam questions and map over the years what areas have come up. You may start to see a pattern with maybe three key areas always occurring and then two areas alternating between the rest of the syllabus. If you only need to answer three questions, you can be fairly certain of revising the three areas that always come up. To be on the safe side, add a final area or two just in case you don't like the way one of the questions is worded. This means that you will be revising 3–5 areas of your syllabus rather than the 8–10 that you will have covered throughout your module.

Some tutors get wise to this and combine topics in questions. You will see if this is the case when you look at past papers. If they do, then there really is no way out of revising the whole syllabus as you don't know what combinations will be together in the exam and hence could end up not knowing half the answers to all the questions.

REVISION LECTURES

Even if you have not attended any lectures throughout the module, make sure you attend the revision lecture. Attendance at lectures is not normally compulsory at university and no register is taken. While it is recommended that you attend lectures if only to gain an overview of the key areas that you need to read around, it is completely up to you.

The revision lecture, however, is absolutely key as this is where you get an indication as to the topic areas that are going to be in the exam, and the sorts of key points that the tutors will be expecting to find in the answers. Academics are not going to waste time going over areas that will not be covered in the exam – they are not trying to catch you out. Academics want you to pass their modules for a number of reasons; firstly, it looks good for them if a module has a high pass rate; secondly, high pass rates mean fewer people doing resits which means less work in the longer run for the academic; finally, academics are human and they like to get some job satisfaction out of motivating students to learn and do well. If everyone did badly in an exam, there would be a lot of questions asked about the module content, the teaching style, the assessment and so forth. Hence it is in the interests of the academic for you to do well. On this basis, academics will give you as much help as possible without actually going so far as cheating.

If at a revision lecture you don't feel the academic is being clear enough – ask them. Ask them if the fact that they haven't covered certain topics means they are unlikely to be in the exam. If they say it is unlikely that anything that wasn't in the lecture is in the exam, then you know you only have to revise what they have covered. Academics will give you as many clues as they can short of telling you the exam questions – you just need to get clever at asking the right questions to collect the clues.

So, the sorts of questions to be asking your lecturers and tutors in revision sessions are:

- Are there any additional topics that you haven't covered in this session that are likely to be in the exam?
- Are any topics combined in the exam, or does each question cover a separate topic? (They may not answer this, but if they do it gives you an idea as to how many topics you need to revise.)
- Are we right in assuming that the topic covered in the assignment does not feature in the exam because it has already been assessed?
- Are there any particular articles, models or theories that we should specifically familiarise ourselves with prior to the exam? (Again they may not answer this, but if there is a question about a specific model, they may tell you which models to look at.)
- Do we have complete choice of questions to answer or are any compulsory? (This again gives you an idea of how many topics you need to cover. If any are compulsory, see if they will tell you which area the compulsory question is in.)

Basically, don't be afraid to ask. Tutors will not answer your questions if they are not able to or if it would make the exam invalid, but they will give you as much help as possible.

REVISING YOUR READING

Hopefully you will have a pile of notes from reading, or a lot of records entered into EndNote by the time you have finished your module and are ready to revise. Unless you have a photographic memory – and for the purposes of this chapter I am going to assume that you do not – then you are unlikely to remember quotes from every reading, or even everything that you have read. Hence it becomes important to prioritise what you are going to try to remember for the exam.

Start off by making a list of the author of the reading, the year, and the key point that is made in the article, chapter or book. Get it down to one sentence. An example is given in Table 8.1 for the start of a reading list on the subject of 'Globalisation of Education'.

Table 8.1 **Reading list on Globalisation of Education**

Author	Year	Key point
Ackroyd & Pilkington	1998	Globalisation compounds children's difficulty to establish their identity as they are identified with a wider range of social strata, often including those taken by the media from global issues.
Amos *et al.*	2002	Globalisation can be dated back to the sixteenth century and can be analysed with regard to the functionality of world markets; the construction of sovereignty and identity; mechanisms of global diffusion; and principles of equality and justice.
Angus	2004	Globalisation has disempowered teachers through the mantra of new managerialism and institutional control impacting on pedagogy and the curriculum.
Ehrenreich	2006	Globalisation has moved from colonialisation, to imperialism, to a form of global relations that benefits a particular group of transnational class.
Forstrop	2007	Globalisation has economic underpinnings as the knowledge economy drives the concept forwards.
Jarvis	2006	Questions whether the nature of the university can be globalised or Europeanised through mechanisms such as the Bologna process.
Marginson	1999	Globalisation is irreversibly changing the politics of the nation state and yet education systems remain grounded in their maintenance.

Source: Adapted from Ford (1992: 220).

Make the list to include everything that you have read. This helps give you an overview of all your reading in the field. Try to read at least one page of the key points part first thing in the morning and last thing at night as this is when your memory is most receptive to retaining ideas.

Now, look at your list of revision topics. Identify the six to eight most useful pieces of reading to meet those topic areas. Ideally, each piece of reading should be able to be used in more than one area. Make a separate list of these key pieces of reading as these are the ones that you will try to remember the authors and years for. So, for example, from the list offered above, the Forstrop (2007) reading could probably be used in a number of essays as he is referring to the economic nature of globalisation generally and linking it to the concept of the knowledge economy. Equally, Marginson (1999) is looking generally at the impact of globalisation on the concept of the nation state. Between these two references you could write answers on the nature of globalisation; the impact of globalisation; globalisation in education; the link between globalisation, education and the economy; and so forth.

Try to be as efficient as possible. Tutors are not going to compare your answers in different subjects. If you manage to use the same reading in different modules then that is a bonus for you. It is allowed, and shows that you can use the literature well, crossing different subject boundaries, and offering a more holistic approach.

REVISING YOUR ASSIGNMENTS

Now, I know I said that the topic area of your assignment should not be in the exam because each learning outcome should only be assessed once – however, you should be able to make use of your assignment in other topic areas. This is back to the principles of efficiency and effectiveness in learning. Don't use something once only – use it for more than one purpose.

Go back to your assignment with a list of the topic areas you are going to be revising. Go through the assignment and make a note of the points that you raised in your assignment that are relevant to each of the topic areas that you are revising. Hopefully, you should find a couple of points of relevance to each.

This is an important exercise to do because you really know the contents of your assignment very well – probably better than you think – so when it comes down to the pressure of the exam, if you can fall back on the learning in your assignment then all the better. Also, it helps you to see how learning can be applied across more than one area or topic.

REVISING TOPIC AREAS

Once you have been through your reading and made your grand list, and you've decided on your topic areas, it is time to start focusing your revision into those areas. Start by sorting your reading by topic area, and the more you can duplicate, the better.

After your reading, look at your assignment and add the key points from your assignment to the pile for each topic area.

Next, go back over your lecture notes and seminar activities. Draw out ideas and examples from these that are relevant to each topic area. Again, the more you can duplicate, the better – and it is important to actually duplicate copying things out, as the more you rewrite or retype something, the more it is likely to become embedded in your memory.

Finally add some examples. Listen to the news with your topic areas in mind. Find some recent examples of items of news that illustrate your topic area. This is another good way of making sure you remember something, and of ensuring that you really understand it. If you can apply the theory of your course to current world events then you are demonstrating to the marking team that you really do understand this topic area. Also, it is easier to remember current examples that are making an impact on our lives, than historical events that lack personal relevance. Remember, you are trying to prepare yourself to perform under exam conditions. The news may not offer you 'the best' example possible, but it is likely to offer you an example you will be able to recall when under pressure.

Using current world affairs in your answer helps demonstrate your skill and understanding to the examiner, without relying on your knowledge. Current affairs are easy to remember as they are likely to be affecting our lives at that time, and they illustrate how you have developed the ability to look at the world now in terms of the studies you are undertaking. This never fails to impress examiners, provided the examples are relevant of course.

PAST EXAM QUESTIONS

The absolute best way of revising – even if you don't follow any of the above suggestions – is to do past exam questions. These allow you to develop your knowledge, and practise the skills of demonstrating understanding as you will have to under exam conditions.

At your first attempt, try to do past questions in the amount of time you will have during your examination – usually 40 minutes per question. See how much you can do in 40 minutes without using your notes or any other aids. Then make yourself a cup of tea and read what you have written – how would you score it? What is missing from it? Now go back to your notes and reading and fill in the gaps. Rewrite the answer with the additions you want to make.

On another day, select a question from a different past paper on the same topic. This time, sit down with your notes and map out what you want to include in the answer. In essence, draw up an essay plan. Now, cover up your notes but not your plan, and set a timer to time how long it takes you to write the essay. Hopefully it will take you less than 40 minutes as you already have the plan laid out on what to write. If it takes you longer than 40 minutes, then keep practising until you can write the essay from the plan in less than 30 minutes.

Now compare the answers from your first and second attempts. How do they differ? What did you leave out of the first answer that you included in the second answer? Make a note of the things that you remembered easily, and the things that you didn't remember to include quite so easily.

On another day, select yet another question from a different past paper – if you've run out of past papers, make some questions up. You should have got a feel for the sorts of questions that will be asked so you should be able to make some up. If not, keep the previous questions but change what you need to do with it, so if it was a 'discuss' question, make it a 'critically evaluate' question.

Now go back to square one with this new question and attempt it without your notes in 40 minutes. Keep repeating the cycle until the answers that you have planned with your notes do not differ much from the answers you write in 40 minutes without notes.

ESSAY PLANS

In many ways writing out an essay plan is as good as writing the essay itself when you are revising. The important element is deciding what you are going to put in the answer, and in what order to structure the answer so that it answers the question coherently.

Some people do plans by doing mind maps, others write keyword lists of what is to go in. There is no correct way of doing a plan. In Chapter 9 I suggest the Ishikawa Fishbone as an outline for a plan when you are actually in the exam as it has advantages over all the other formats in the exam itself.

Being able to write an essay plan is a key skill for passing an exam as it evidences your ability to think quickly and clearly, link concepts and ideas together, draw on evidence and examples, and order your thoughts to form a cohesive argument in a short space of time.

You could even generate generic essay plans for each topic area you are revising as there will be certain elements that are likely to be relevant to any question or title. These elements will include definition of terms, key theorists in the field, key models of the topic area, and current examples of the theory in practice. If you can learn your generic essay plan then all you have to do in the exam is link it to the question being asked.

REVISION FOR MULTIPLE CHOICE EXAMS

There is a perception that multiple choice exams are easier than essays. This is true to a degree as you don't start with a blank page – you start with a list of answers, one of which you know is going to be the right answer. However, multiple choice questions can be written in such a way that they are very tricky indeed, with the nuance of the answer changing with one word. Well written multiple choice questions can be very difficult to answer unless you know your subject area in much more detail than would be necessary for an essay exam.

Make sure you practise previous multiple choice exams prior to sitting yours, and analyse past papers in terms of how the questions are phrased and presented. Does your examiner differentiate between individual words such as 'sufficient' and 'necessary' in questions? Does your examiner differentiate between past and present tense within the same question? These are all tricks that test your attention to detail and how carefully you are reading the question.

REVISION GROUPS

Some people find it very difficult to concentrate when revising, and revising with others can help this. However, it is important to be disciplined about this rather than simply wasting time chatting. Past exam questions can also be a very good way of focusing revision groups. You could all have a bash at writing an answer prior to the revision group meeting. If you are feeling brave you could then swap scripts within the group and mark each other's, otherwise just talk through your own.

Comparing and contrasting what you put in your answers is a good way of getting to grips with what could be included in an answer, what works well and what doesn't work so well. You could then try to draw up the model answer plan between you.

Revision groups work best when they focus on answering questions or discussing what you have learnt about particular topics. Preparing something in advance is key, otherwise the group degenerates into talking about how little you all know rather than what you actually do know.

If your revision group meets for an hour and there are four of you, the sort of agenda you might put forward could be something like this:

5 mins – intro and update

5 mins each – round robin of what you put in your answer to the practice question completed in advance

10 mins – compare answers for similarities and differences

10 mins – explore the differences

10 mins – develop new ideas for additions, e.g. current examples from the news

5 mins – agree next practice question and time of next meeting

Set a group timetable to ensure you cover all the topics that you need to prior to the exam, and circulate past papers so that you can agree which questions to tackle. Keep the other questions to practise on your own, both before and after the group meeting. The revision group should be one element of your revision strategy, not the only element. You need to do more than just discuss your answers to questions with others, although the discussion is valuable and can add a lot to the revision process, if only in terms of keeping you motivated.

REVISION TIMETABLE

You should definitely have one week clear for revision, and if you are lucky with the timing of your exams, you may have two weeks for revision. It is important to use this time wisely. Going back to the timetable created for your average week in Chapter 3, this can be reworked for your revision timetable into something like the example shown in Table 8.2 opposite.

This becomes a very busy week but you only get one crack at your exams so it is important to make the best of it. If you fail, you get to resit once, but you can only achieve a basic pass mark which prevents you from failing your degree, but doesn't contribute well to the classification of your degree.

Note that the timetable stops most nights at 8 or 9pm. This is to allow you to wind down, relax, work out any stress and then get a good night's sleep. Remember those Olympic athletes – diet and sleep are key components in the run-up to a strong performance.

Equally, first thing in the morning and last thing at night, read your list of key points from your reading, or look at one of your diagrams, or something that you need to try to remember. Some people's memories take the last thing they concentrate on into their subconscious when they go to sleep. If you are one of those people, don't miss the opportunity – and if it doesn't work that strongly for you, it won't hurt or harm you either.

Table 8.2 **Revision timetable**

Time	Monday	Tuesday	Wednesday	Thursday	Friday	Saturday	Sunday
9–10	Practice question topic 1	Revise reading and notes topic 2	Revise reading and notes topic 3	Job at Tesco	Revise reading and notes	Job at Tesco	Revise reading and past questions all topics
10–11	Revision group meeting topic 1				Essay plan topic 4		
11–12	Essay plan topic 1	Practice question topic 2	Shopping for exam provisions		Practice question topic 4		
12–1	Revise reading topic 1	Essay plan topic 2	Washing		Revise diagram for links between topics		Bar job
1–2		Compare & contrast topics 1 & 2	Lazy lunch				
2–3	Practice question topic 1		Revise reading and notes topic 4		Practice question topic 3		
3–4	Essay plan topic 1	Revise assignments for common themes			Revision group meeting topic 4		
4–5	Diagram of content for topic 1			Review 3 topics for overlap	Revision group review overlap ideas		
5–6		Revision group meeting topic 2	Revision group meeting topic 3 and re-run topics 1 & 2	Practice question topic 4			Practice exam questions – whole paper from year 3
6–7	Bar job			Map overlap between 4 topics in diagram form	Bar job		
7–8		Practice question topic 2				Re-read notes from reading	
8–9							Review answers

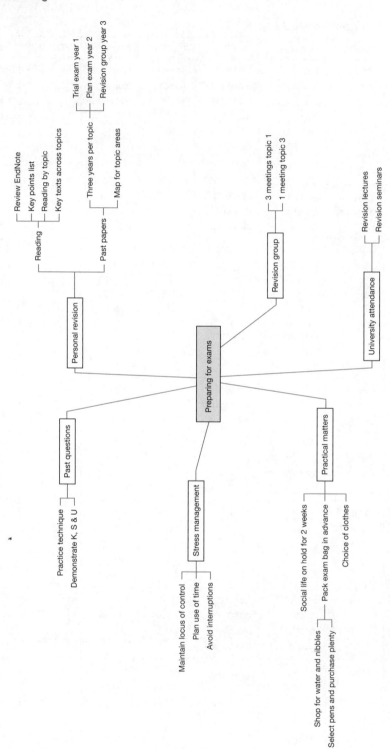

Figure 8.1 Preparing for exams mind map

RESTRUCTURING YOUR KNOWLEDGE

Given that an exam is not meant to be a memory test but your ability to construct an argument to answer a question under exam conditions, it can help some people to find different ways of expressing their knowledge and understanding. For example, some people find it useful to map their understanding of a topic area as a mind map.

A mind map allows you to put the topic area in the centre, and then related key points linking to it, and then points that support those key points linking back, and so forth.

An example of a mind map on preparation for exams is given in Figure 8.1.

Alternatively, you might find it useful to draw a Venn diagram of three topic areas you are revising, and map how the relevant theories, ideas and authors might relate to each. A simple example of this for introductory Human Resource Management is given in Figure 8.2.

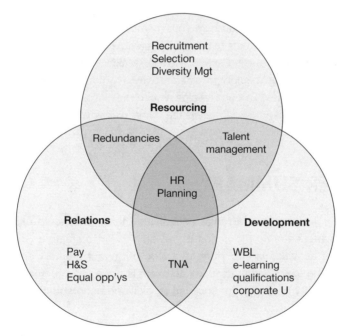

Figure 8.2 Diagram illustrating how revision areas can overlap allowing you to use the same theory to support more than one subject area

Can you see how this might help you identify which authors you could use for more than one topic area? Some people have visual memories. If you do, you will find it easier to recall this diagram in your exam than you will the list generated from your reading. If you find it easier to remember diagrams than text, then draw diagrams for your revision.

A BIT ABOUT MEMORY

Just in case you are starting to lose faith as your exams approach and you think that the advice is not working, here is the theory to underpin the range of activities that should be involved in revision.

There are three stages in the memory process: acquisition, storage and retrieval (Melton, 1963). Acquisition applies to the initial learning and this is what the re-reading of notes helps with. This stage is about making sure that you have acquired what you need to remember in the first place. Storage is the invisible bit about the brain's system holding items and them decaying over time. Retrieval is the process by which we get at and use the information we have stored, and this is covered in the exam preparation phase by doing past questions.

In the 'invisible bit' – the storage element – we have a both short term and long term memory (Atkinson & Shiffrin, 1971). Rehearsing things, coding things, making decisions about things, and frequently retrieving things help move 'things' from short term to longer term memory. Rehearsing involves going over the same thing again and again. Repetition can help your memory. Coding involves making links and connections between items to help you remember them better and this is where drawing diagrams and making links can help. Making decisions involves you in reviewing items in your memory in different ways so that you use them to make judgements and choices. This again helps embed the ideas. Frequent retrieval stops you from forgetting as you keep using the same pieces of information again and again.

CHAPTER SUMMARY

This chapter has outlined a range of activities that you should endeavour to undertake when entering the period of 'revision' prior to sitting an examination. The range of activities is important as it aids both your memory and your performance in the examination itself, as an exam is not a strict memory test, but a test of your ability to apply your knowledge, skill and understanding under exam conditions.

BUSINESS GAME

The organisation has been invited on to a TV business chat show where the host is wanting to discuss with a panel of three international development managers the ethics, marketing and corporate governance of their international activities. You have been told by your MD that you will represent the organisation on this programme, and need to 'mug up' on the areas concerned. How will you go about preparing for the 30-minute chat show?

You have been told specifically that the areas will be ethics, marketing and corporate governance. Make sure you have learned the company line on these areas in advance and, if necessary, take supporting documentation with you to read off. Other topics you might want to look at include company finances, as profitability is often a question when it comes to internationalisation. There may be other items as well that you think you might need to know, and indeed things that the company might want you to get across. Choose your topic areas well, and revise, rehearse, and talk to anyone and everyone to practise articulating your ideas succinctly.

References

Ackroyd, J. & Pilkington, A. (1998) Globalisation, childhood and the production of ethnic identities. *Social Science Teacher,* 28(1), 11–16.

Amos, S. K., Keiner, E., Proske, M. & Radtke, R.-O. (2002) Globalisation: autonomy of education under siege? Shifting boundaries between politics, economy and education. *European Educational Research Journal,* 1(2), 193–213.

Angus, L. (2004) Globalization and educational change: bringing about the reshaping and re-norming of practice. *Journal of Education Policy,* 19(1), 23–41.

Atkinson, R. C. & Shiffrin, R. M. (1971) The control of short-term memory. *Scientific American*, 224, 83–89.

Ehrenreich, T. (2006) Globalisation: a personal view. In K. April & M. Shockley (Eds.), *Diversity: New realities in a changing world* (pp. 66–81). Hampshire: Palgrave.

Forstrop, P.-A. (2007) Who's colonizing who? The knowledge society thesis and the global challenges in higher education. *Studies in Philosophy of Education,* 27, 227–236.

Jarvis, P. (2006) The Bologna Process: Europeanisation or globalisation? *Prospero,* 12(1), 6–13.

Marginson, S. (1999) After globalization: emerging politics of education. *Journal of Education Policy,* 14(1), 19–31.

Melton, A. W. (1963) Implications of short-term memory for a general theory of memory. *Journal of Verbal Learning and Verbal Behaviour*, 2, 1–21.

9 ▸ PASSING WRITTEN EXAMINATIONS

This chapter focuses on what to do in the actual examination itself. Basically, this chapter is the key chapter on how to pass exams, offering you a technique that has helped many 'failing' students turn results into successes.

This chapter will cover:

■ A technique to help you pass exams

■ Separation of hand and brain

■ Time management within the examination hall itself

USING THIS CHAPTER

INTRODUCTION

This chapter introduces you to a technique that has helped hundreds of students pass exams who previously used to fail them. If you take nothing else from this book, try to follow this technique. Combine it with Chapter 8 on revision and exam failure should become a thing of the past. The trick to passing exams is not being clever or having a good memory, it is about demonstrating technique under pressure. This chapter will teach you an exam technique that can be applied to any examination where there is the requirement to write essays or some form of answer in prose.

TECHNIQUE 1 – DIVISION OF LABOUR

Back in Chapter 6 there was a discussion about why people fail exams and a number of lessons were drawn out. These included not answering the question set, writing too much on one point, going off at a tangent, poor time management, and so forth. Most of these occur because the student's brain takes over their hand and they get into a stream of writing what the brain is telling them to write. Given that most of us hardly use handwriting at all these days because most work is done on our computers, writing for 2–3 hours at a time is also strenuous and can lead to cramp and sore hands. There is an easy answer to all of these problems – division of labour.

Separate hand from brain. Do not think and write at the same time. Separate the tasks of thinking and writing.

At first sight this looks crazy. If you're not thinking when you are writing then you will write garbage. Actually the opposite is true for most people in exams. When they do think while they write they write garbage because they are trying to think ahead as well as think about the bit they are writing at that point in time. So, how do you separate hand from brain? Write a plan first, the brain bit, and then write the essay, the hand bit.

TECHNIQUE 2 – THE ISHIKAWA FISHBONE

In the 1980's a Japanese Management Guru called Kaoru Ishikawa pioneered a cause and effect quality management process which he represented using a fishbone diagram. This fishbone outline lends itself perfectly to essay plans in exams, although it has nothing to do with quality management. In fact, there is nothing about Ishikawa's theory that applies to exams at all – but his fishbone is just perfect. Why? For a number of reasons.

Firstly, it only allows for a number of bones in the fish, or strands/themes in the answer. This makes you focus on what you really want to say.

Secondly, once you have identified your key themes, you can then add flesh to the bones. This allows you to put detail into your plan.

Thirdly, even if you feel you know nothing, drawing the fishbone and adding an introduction and conclusion starts to fill the fishbone up, and this makes you feel like you do know something. By drawing on your self-efficacy, the fishbone helps you believe that you can write this essay and hence you do.

Finally, the fishbone then gives you the perfect essay plan so that you can then write your essay without having to engage your brain, quickly, efficiently, and with perfectly executed division of labour. A blank fishbone is presented in Figure 9.1.

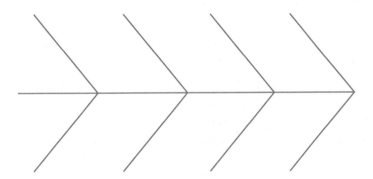

Figure 9.1 **Blank fishbone template**

The basic idea of the fishbone is that you have eight key bones in your essay. One is the introduction and one is the conclusion. This leaves you with a maximum of six key issues to put into your essay. We will come to populating the fishbone later, but before you start on your fishbone, there is something else you need to do.

TECHNIQUE 3 – WRITE OUT THE TITLE

Most students don't believe me when I tell them this can be the make or break point of an exam. Even if you master all of the other techniques, if you slip up on this one you will fail.

Most people fail exams because they do not answer the question set. They answer a variation of the question set, usually because in their rush to get started they do not read the question properly.

I have never yet seen anyone fail an exam for not answering the question set when they have written out the question. An essay title takes maybe a minute to copy out.

While you copy it down you say it to yourself at least a dozen times. Your brain starts thinking about what you are saying, and you focus on the question asked.

Writing out the question also serves to slow you down. It makes you stop, take breath, and do something basic that everyone can do – copying out. Hence you have your first small step of success. You have correctly read and written down the question. Don't underestimate how important that is. Remember, the number one reason people fail exams is they don't answer the question set.

TECHNIQUE 4 – ENGAGING THE BRAIN

Having written out the question and drawn your blank fishbone, your page is no longer blank but is starting to look like you might be a student that knows something. Now it is time to populate the fishbone.

The first bone and the last bone are easy. The first bone is the introduction. In this you are going to define the key terms in the title so that the marker knows that you know what you are talking about. This also gives clarity to the answer.

The last bone is going to be the conclusion. This is where you are going to sum up your argument to answer the question. Therefore, at this point in time, you know what you will be concluding. It will either be a discussion in which case you will conclude as to the key points; or it will be a compare and contrast in which case you will conclude on similarities and differences; or it will be to evaluate or critically evaluate in which case you will be making a judgement value as to how well the issue being examined meets the need identified.

Representing this on the fishbone is a question of naming your bones and then starting to put some 'flesh' on them. Let's take an example of a compare and contrast essay – the fishbone would start to look like the example given in Figure 9.2.

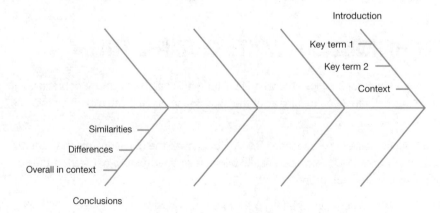

Figure 9.2 **Fishbone with introduction and conclusions outlined**

In some ways, compare and contrast essays are easy because you know you only have to consider two main ideas. In a discussion essay, the field may be more open, but again just concentrate on the key terms in the title and define them in the introduction. In your conclusions you might want to present arguments for or against the idea being discussed and then again concluding finally in the context of the title.

So, you have your introduction and your conclusions, now you need to put more meat on the fish. The next obvious point is to think about key theories, models or ideas that underpin the terms that have been defined in your introduction. Hence you are likely to have a bone for each term, which will be fleshed out with the theories or ideas that are behind them. Now your fishbone should resemble Figure 9.3.

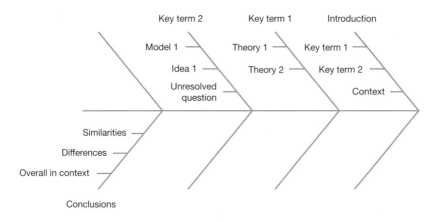

Figure 9.3 **Populating the fishbone with key terms and models**

Now your essay plan is really starting to take shape. You've defined your terms in your introduction and set them in the context of what the question has asked. You've then gone on to identify the key theories, ideas, models and any outstanding unresolved issues that remain with those key terms. Now you can get down to the business of comparing and contrasting them. This will fill another two bones, leaving you two more to fill. A good working example can be a means of filling empty bones, or areas of dispute, or any issues that might be impacting on the question from external sources. These can then be drawn into the plan as shown in Figure 9.4.

Now your fishbone is starting to look like a seriously good essay. All you have to do is write it! Practise doing fishbones as part of your revision when you do past questions as outlined in Chapter 8. You should become quite skilled at them. Don't worry if you think the bones are in the wrong order – when you have finished your plan simply number them in order in which you will then write them in the essay.

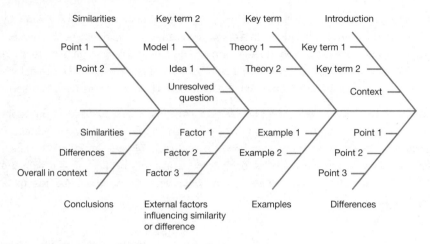

Figure 9.4 Complete fishbone essay plan

In terms of division of time, most students who get skilled at this find they can spend up to half of their time working out their fishbone and then spend the other half of the time writing the essay. Others prefer to spend 15 minutes on the fishbone and then 25 minutes writing – it depends on how fast a writer you are.

TECHNIQUE 5 – ENGAGING THE HAND

The reason you can spend up to half the time doing the fishbone plan is that the writing job is now very straightforward and quick. For each piece of flesh on the bone you are simply going to write a three sentence paragraph. Each sentence has the following content:

1 Sentence 1 introduces the concept; for example 'X introduced theory 1 to the field mid twentieth century as part of the Factor 1 movement.'

2 Sentence 2 explains the contribution of the concept; for example 'This made people question the value of what they were doing with respect to Y and brought about a political shift in favour of Factor 1.'

3 Sentence 3 then links this back to the title: for example, 'This contrasts with the ideas of key term 2 because key term 2 is fundamentally opposed to Factor 1.'

Now move on to the next paragraph and start this routine again. As a marker we find ourselves going tick, tick, tick, down the margin. You've made your point. You've linked it to the title to ensure you are answering the question set. You don't need to tell us anything more. Move on.

You need to time yourself and practise writing these three sentence paragraphs so that you allow yourself enough time when you are in the exam to write your essay.

TECHNIQUE 6 – STRICT TIME MANAGEMENT

Remember that stress management and time management are not mutually exclusive. If you carefully manage your time, your stress levels will reduce, and you will be giving yourself the best opportunity of scoring the maximum marks across all the questions.

Let's say for example that you have a two hour exam in which you need to write three essays out of a possible six, all carrying an equal weighting with regard to the marks distribution. Your timetable for the exam period should therefore be as follows:

---

5 mins – read the paper and decide on the best three essays to answer and in which order

15 mins – write out title of essay 1; complete fishbone plan

20 mins – write essay 1

15 mins – write out title of essay 2; complete fishbone plan

20 mins – write essay 2

15 mins – write out title of essay 3; complete fishbone plan

20 mins – write essay 3

5 mins – read back through answers adding any key points that additionally spring to mind while re-reading

5 mins – make sure you have completed the front of the exam answer book correctly with your details and the question numbers you have answered in the order that you answered them.

The reason for leaving the admin of the front of your answer book to last is that most invigilators will let you finish doing this when time is up, so don't panic if you haven't completed it all when the time is up. It isn't really part of the exam itself, more the record of who you are and what you have done.

You do not have to write your answers in the order that they appear in the exam paper. You can choose which order to answer the questions in, but you must record this clearly on the front of the answer book. Start off with the question that you think you know the most about. This gives you confidence that you have got one good answer down before you move on, and it allows you to dump a lot of what is in your brain down on paper quite quickly, freeing up your memory to recall matters relating to later questions. Also, you may find you get through this question quicker than you've allowed time for which gives you additional time for the other questions.

It doesn't matter if you finish your essay early and move on. The golden rule though is that you do not spend more than the time allowed on a question. If you finish a later question quickly you can always go back – but don't overrun as you progress through the paper. Get to the end of the paper and then go back.

If you think you might add more, you can either leave a page or two blank in the exam book for additions, or you can add a note directing the marker as to where to go to find the additional bit for that essay. So long as you clearly indicate that you have continued later in the book by (*1) for example, then the examiner will look for (*1) and continue marking.

TECHNIQUE 7 – STICK TO THE GAME PLAN

If while you are engaging your hand rather than your brain you suddenly think of something else that should go in the essay – stop writing and go and mark it as an addition on the fishbone. Then start writing again where you left off.

By doing this you get it out of your brain which allows you to concentrate on writing again but also gives you the reassurance that you have written it down somewhere so you don't need to try to remember it. It also prevents you going off at a tangent.

Stick to the game plan. Do not be tempted to deviate under pressure. You will gain fewer marks for making an addition to a previous essay than you will from starting the next. This is also why you should not overrun on any single essay as you progress through your exam. Stop when the allocated time is up and move on. Come back to it later if you have time at the end.

TECHNIQUE 8 – SPACE YOUR WORK OUT

No matter how environmentally friendly you are, now is not the time to try to save paper. If a marker cannot read your writing you are not going to pass, no matter how good the content is. One thing that really helps is leaving a line between each line you write on, as if you were double-line spacing in your word processor. Even neat handwriting becomes easier to read when double-line spaced, and messy, large handwriting becomes legible.

Do your fishbone plan on a whole page. Then start your essay on the next page – double line spaced. When you have finished your essay, leave a page or two, and then move on to the next essay. You do not get charged for using lots of paper in an exam so don't try to be economical. You can use as many answer books as you need – just make sure they all have your identifier number and the question number on them and that they are collated together at the end in the correct order.

MULTIPLE CHOICE TECHNIQUE

Often people think that multiple choice exams are easier to pass. There is an element of truth to that if you are lucky, in that one of the answers presented is right so there is a chance that with a complete guess you could get the right answer. Answering 'A' all the way through the paper is likely to get you 20–25 per cent of the marks and I have seen students do that when they really don't feel they know the answer to anything. This said, to do well in a multiple choice exam you need to know your subject area in much more detail and depth than would be necessary to do well in an essay exam.

Well constructed multiple choice questions are not easy to answer. Often all four or five of the answers given could be correct for the topic area being examined, but only one is correct for the specific way in which that question is worded. Hence it is very important to read the question at least twice to make sure you have read it correctly and understand it. Sometimes writing down the keywords can help you focus on what the question is really asking. Some people like to underline keywords in the question; others reword the question in the margin thinking what is this question really asking me?

Just as with essays, one of the prime reasons people fail multiple choice exams is because they haven't understood the question properly and hence answer the wrong question. This is different to not knowing the right answer. Not understanding what the question is asking is a key problem, so you cannot spend too long reading the question.

Only once you feel you understand the question should you go on to look at the answers. Some answers will strike you immediately as being wrong for the question. Strike those ones out so that you reduce the number of possible correct answers. If you're lucky, you'll identify all but one as being wrong – that leaves you with the correct answer.

Note that we are looking for those that are wrong first rather than those that are right. It is easier to convince yourself that an answer might be right than it is to see it as wrong. If you know something is wrong, then you can be pretty sure that you are right about that. If you think something is right, you might think the same about the next one, and the next one and so on. Hence making negative judgements first to reduce down the field of possible right answers works for most people.

Now you probably have two or three answers left that might possibly be the right one. Read the question again and then read your first choice of possible answer. Then read the question again and the second possible answer, and so forth until you have considered each possible answer against the question. You might note another as being wrong and cross it off the list.

If you have two answers that are very similar left as your possibles, look at what the difference is between the answers and try to eliminate that difference by re-reading the question and considering the point of difference. Which way do you go? Again it can be easier to think about which way the difference is most wrong rather than fits best.

To a large extent the skill of answering multiple choice questions is not to know what the right answer is, but to know why the other answers are wrong. Often the right answer has been cleverly worded in such a way that it doesn't strike you as being the right answer when you first read it. Often it focuses on a peripheral tangent that wouldn't be the natural thing to think of when you first read the question. Don't discount answers until you are sure they are wrong. Don't jump to conclusions too quickly. Take your time, read the question a number of times to check that you've read it and understood it correctly, and then consider the answers available.

SHORT ANSWER QUESTIONS

If you have an exam paper with a section which has short answer questions, often with each carrying a different weighting of marks, then you need to vary the length of answer in accordance with the number of marks the question carries. A question for six marks will require more material in its answer than a question for two marks which may require only one or two points to be made.

This sort of section can be difficult to time manage as you don't want to waste time allocating time between the questions according to their spread of marks, but equally you want to make sure you give a ten mark answer longer than a four mark answer. Hence you have to be quite aware of time as you progress through such a section.

Depending on how the question is asked, you may not have to answer in sentences. For example, if the questions asks 'State two factors that might impact on your ability to pass this exam?' you could answer simply 'ability to think under pressure and time management'. This takes much less time to write than 'Two factors that might impact on my ability to pass this exam are my ability to think under pressure and my time management.' Equally, the question just asks you to 'state' them; it doesn't ask you explain how they might impact on your ability to pass this exam and hence no explanation should be given because you won't gain extra marks for it.

Use of bullet points can help you structure answers in short questions without reverting to sentences while clearly differentiating that you are making another point. Ideally you want to try to have as many bullet points as there are marks available.

In terms of time management, allocate the amount of time you have to spend on the short answer question section and when that time is up, move on. You can always go back and answer more at the end if you have time to spare but you need to move on to the essay section or you won't leave yourself enough time.

Always show your workings out in your answer book. Often short answer sections appear in subject areas where there are calculations, formulae or diagrams to be used. If you show the marker how you were making the calculation, if you go wrong at the final step, you can get credit for the bits you did right. If you simply record the final answer and it is wrong then you will score zero for that question.

Finally, don't panic if you don't know the answer to a question. If a particular question throws you, simply skip it and move on to the next one. It is not worth wasting time on a question for a few marks when you can pick up the marks elsewhere. You are not expected to remember everything or know everything. The examiner will not be expecting you to score 100 per cent in this section so you shouldn't hold that expectation of yourself. Don't worry about not knowing a question – move on.

CHAPTER SUMMARY

This chapter outlines a disciplined approach to passing exams that leaves little to chance by mastering technique. Of course as a student you do need to know something about what you are writing about; but the techniques offered in this chapter prevent you from suffering the fate of failure outlined in Chapter 6. These techniques are not instantly learnt – they take practice. You need to become so familiar with them that they become the natural thing for you to do when you feel under stress to produce an answer quickly. They help you structure your thoughts, build your confidence that you do know something with regard to the answer, and build your self-efficacy in terms of your ability to pass the exam. Practice makes perfect. Students who practise this can get to the point where they spend half the time engaging the brain and half engaging the hand – and it never ceases to amaze them that they need so little time to write if they've got the thinking right in the first place.

BUSINESS GAME

You now manage a team of five people who look after each continent respectively. You get the group together to try to share some learning and draw out key lessons for new product and new market launches. You want to see how each person's ideas differ initially before they merge into group think. How might you do this?

You could set them a question in advance with a fishbone diagram for them to populate. By comparing and contrasting the diagrams, a multitude of learning and ideas could be generated taking the group forward in terms of the way it works together and the way it approaches the regions of the world.

10 ▶ THE EXAMINATION POST-MORTEM

This chapter helps you learn from feedback and when things haven't gone as well as had been hoped. It is true that we can learn from our mistakes, but we actually have to stop and reflect on them in order to be able to do so, otherwise we are likely to make the same mistakes again and again.

This chapter will cover:

- How to learn from your successes and failures
- How to take learning forward from one event to another
- Planning for your future after you leave university

USING THIS CHAPTER

INTRODUCTION

This chapter focuses on how to use each year's exam experience to build positively for the next year through structured reflection. As this is the final chapter on exams it also helps you reflect on what you want to do next, where you want your career to go, and how to think about your future development ... with maybe a little plug for further university study!

IMMEDIATELY POST-EXAM

The worst thing you can possibly do immediately after an exam is go through with your friends what you put in each question. It becomes a point-scoring exercise with everyone trying to make themselves feel better at the expense of everyone else, and actually leaves everyone feeling worse as it is unlikely that you will have put the same things in your answers so you start doubting what you put, and you'll suddenly realise what you forgot to put in that others did. By the end of the chat you've decided you've failed and go home depressed. It is a waste of time, energy and emotion.

Once you have left an examination hall, you cannot do anything to change the mark you are going to get as your answer is written and final. You'll experience a mixture of relief that it is over, exhaustion from the physical effort of writing for so long and the mental effort of answering the questions, and emptiness because 'what next?'

This last feeling is particularly strong if you have just finished your final exams. Your life has been so busy with studying and suddenly it is over – and it is amazing how many hours there are in a day with nothing to do.

So, when you come out of the examination hall, either go out and party, go home and prepare for your next exam, or go and do something which has nothing at all to do with your studies. You are allowed to write some notes for later on of what you put in your answers – but don't share them with anyone – use them for a structured post-mortem later on. Do no more than complete the exam review sheet opposite.

EXAM REVIEW SHEET

	Key points written in question in exam
Q1	
Q2	
Q3	
Q4	

EXAM REVIEW SHEET continued

	Key issues regarding technique to review
Choice of questions	
Type of answer required	
Memory recall	
Time management	
Essay plans	
Division of labour	
Other	

DEVELOPING THE REFLECTIVE PRACTITIONER

The concept of the reflective practitioner is usually linked in some way to Donald Schon and his 1983 work *The Reflective Practitioner*. Schon came up with the concepts of reflection-on-action and reflection-in-action. Reflection-on-action is the technically rational idea of looking back at something and analysing it, much as outlined in the next three sections in this chapter. Reflection-in-action, on the other hand, is the ability to reflect as an experience is occurring so that you can modify or change the experience. It is a form of 'thinking on your feet' that requires you actually to reflect back and put yourself in touch with learning, experience, emotions, or recollections of similar occurrences that then allow you to alter the current occurrence to reach a different outcome. It is not 'chance'. It is a deliberate process that your mind goes through that allows you to reflect while you are having an experience so that you can change, rather than reflecting after the experience so that you can learn. However, in order to be able to do the former, you need to have done the latter. That is, you need to have the learning from reflecting back in order to be able to reflect during.

Once you have mastered reflection-on-action you become more than a rationalist and more of an artist as you apply your learning-in-action to make a difference to outcomes as they occur. With regard to examinations this means that if you can learn from one exam to the other with regard to your technique, then you can change your technique as you go through an exam to achieve a more favourable outcome.

STRUCTURED POST-MORTEM TO AID REFLECTION

Do not look back at an exam until you have your result. Until you know whether or not your effort scored well or not, there is no point in looking back at it. Once you have your mark, you can go back and analyse what you did that gained you the points, and what you may have missed out that resulted in the mark being lower than it might have been. Remember, you do not 'lose' marks, you only gain them so don't think about where you lost marks, think about where you may have been able to gain more.

Once you have your mark, go back to any notes you took out of the exam hall (if any), or think back to the exam paper, and outline what you put in your answer – you could even draw another fishbone. Now go back to your notes and see if there were additional points that you could have made to add more flesh to the bones.

	Areas of good performance	Areas for improvement
Q1		
Q2		
Q3		
Q4		

If you are really struggling to see why your mark is not what you had anticipated, go and talk to your tutor. Most universities do not give feedback on exam scripts, nor do they allow you to see your exam script after it has been marked, as much for administrative reasons as anything else – but you can go and talk to your tutor, taking along your notes, and go through with them why you might not have gained as many marks as you had wanted. Remember, everyone is trying to help you pass as well as you can, so ask for feedback and help if you need to.

The most important thing is that you learn from the examination experience for the next time. Did you get your time management right – if not, note this for next time. Did you write a conclusion that linked back to the title – if not, note this for next time. Did you go off at a tangent to the question being asked – if so, note this for next time so you don't do it again. It is too late to do anything about the exam you have just sat, all you can do is take the learning forward in a positive way to the next time.

LEARNING FROM DISAPPOINTING RESULTS (REFLECTION-ON-ACTION)

It can be very disheartening to do badly in an exam, particularly if you fail outright as you then have to do the same thing again in a second effort to pass, which adds to the stress. This is why it is vitally important to find out why you did badly the first time round. Once you know the causes of the issue you can do something to redress them – otherwise you are likely to do just as badly second time round.

Once you have worked out what the issues were that led to your poor performance you can work out a corrective action plan to address the issues. Make sure that you practise the issues that were the problem. If it was lack of time, practise answering the set number of questions in the time allowed; if it was poor memory, get someone to test you on the facts so that you practise recalling them; if it was badly structured answers, practise writing fishbone plans and the essays that result from them; if you didn't answer the question asked, practise writing concluding paragraphs for each type of question that might be asked so that you know how to end an answer that is a 'discuss' or a 'compare and contrast', or a 'critically evaluate'. Don't leave it to chance hoping you get it right second time round because you won't. Technique takes practice and an awful lot of doing well in exams is technique.

Reason for poor performance	Remedial action to be undertaken	Timetable for remedial action

Finally, don't try to find some external factor to blame for your disappointing result. This goes back to the internal locus of control issue – it is you that did badly, nobody else. So it is not the fault of the exam paper that you chose to revise the wrong subjects; it is not the fault of the people sitting next to you that you couldn't keep your concentration; it is not the fault of the invigilator that you didn't manage to keep time; it is your fault. Once you acknowledge this, you can do something about it. Take ownership of the issue and you can do something about it – otherwise you are leaving your future to chance.

LEARNING FROM GOOD RESULTS (REFLECTION-ON-ACTION)

As much can be learnt from success as from failure. Stop to think about why you did well so that you can replicate it again in your next set of exams. Equally, if you didn't do well but you know someone who did, ask them about their technique so that you can learn from them. They should be flattered and it will be good for them also to go through how they perform actually in the examination hall.

Again, with your success, try to locate what it is that you did that led to your success rather than you simply 'being lucky'. If you were in control of your success then you can replicate it; if it was outside circumstances then you are still leaving your future to chance.

Go back through the exam thinking about how you tackled each question; how you managed your time; how you stopped yourself from panicking or getting too stressed; how you organised your answers; how you recalled the key points to put in the answers; and so forth. These techniques will not have happened by chance, you just might not realise how you did them at the time, so it is worth spending the time going back over the experience and drawing out the learning, both to embed it to ensure you do the same next time, and to improve your technique even further.

Reason for good performance	Remedial action to be undertaken	Timetable for remedial action

IMPROVING PERFORMANCE AT YOUR NEXT EXAMS (REFLECTION-IN-ACTION)

Having analysed what went wrong last time, and practised your technique to ensure that you have mastered the various elements for this next set of exams, all you now need to do is put it into practice. No matter how much you practise, you cannot replicate the discomfort of the exam conditions themselves, because even if you lock yourself in a room for two hours, it is two hours of your choice, and not an enforced two hours imposed by an invigilator.

The build-up to the start of an exam also adds to rather than detracts from nerves – the sitting watching the clock until it reaches the hour so that you can start. The waiting around outside the exam hall with everyone cramming in last-minute revision – none of which does any good. If you don't know your subject by that point, it really is too late. All the bags and coats at the front of the room, with people suddenly remembering that they haven't switched off their mobile phones. This is the time to stay calm and focused. Concentrate on your breathing and keep it slow and regular. Keep telling yourself that you are ready, and focus on positive thoughts rather than worries.

Once the exam starts remind yourself to stick to the game plan, and every 15 minutes or so just take a second to check that you have stuck to the game plan and that you are not making the same mistakes as last time. If you do find yourself wandering from the game plan, notice this and change it. This is the time for reflection-in-action, so that you are reviewing what you are doing with a view to changing this if it is not what you want to be doing.

WHAT NEXT? NO MORE EXAMS!

The good news is that for most Masters level qualifications, and for all doctoral qualifications, there are no exams! Professional bodies do tend to have exams as they are quite literally testing you as to your ability to join the profession, and MBAs tend to have exams as they are accredited by various bodies around the world and can count towards professional exams also. Beyond that, most Masters qualifications use alternative forms of assessment such as assignments, projects, dissertations or presentations. You should certainly be able to tell from the prospectus which Masters do have exams so you can avoid those ones if you really don't ever want to do another written exam.

You may find that once you leave university and start work that you are a bit bored. Work is okay, it offers certain challenges, but you may miss the intellectual challenge of studying, if only to have an argument for the sake of having an argument.

Some of you may wish to continue with your studies part time quite quickly after starting your career while you still have the discipline of studying techniques fresh in your mind. This is great and gets you ahead in terms of your career progression, but equally taking some time out to experience life is also worthwhile. It doesn't really matter when you return to studying, it is just good that you do.

PROFESSIONAL CAREERS

For most 'professional' careers, your degree is not going to be the final studying you do. Most professional bodies have a qualification which is required in order to become a member of the professional body itself, and this is seen as the gateway into the profession. For some professions, such as doctors and teachers, the professional exam is a statutory requirement of entry and you are not allowed to practise in that profession without it. You must also then register with the professional body which can strike you off the register if you do not maintain professional standards and conduct.

Other professional bodies are more gatekeepers to entry to the profession, such as the Chartered Institute of Personnel and Development (CIPD) which has an amazingly onerous set of qualifications that they've put in place as an entry to the HR profession – and it is difficult to get a good job in HR without qualified membership of the institute. However, with this type of institute, other courses, such as Masters in HRM can get you exemption from the professional exams, and hence there are more entry routes than might first seem apparent.

Professional careers also require that you undertake continuous professional development (CPD) on an annual basis, so even if you only do short courses, you'll still come back to studying for at least a couple of days every year.

DEVELOPING A LOVE OF LEARNING

Learning should be infectious. If you look at a small child they are trying to touch and play with everything as they learn; they want to learn from everything they see. As we grow older, that desire to learn seems to drop away – possibly due to the rigidity of the testing and examination system we have in school and university. Once you get past your undergraduate degree, learning can become great fun again, as you move into research which is new learning about new things, and nothing is more exciting.

While you may leave your degree thinking 'never again', don't write off studying forever. You may find in another 15 years' time that you are bored with your career and want a change and come back to studying for a whole new purpose.

Alternatively you may have children that motivate you to take up learning again, or you may find you hit a career plateau unless you take the next step up in qualifications. Whatever the reason, come back with an open mind and a willingness to learn. Postgraduate study is very different to undergraduate study, and is generally undertaken when you are in a much better place in life – your own home, a career, an income that allows a decent diet and heating, and so on.

CONTINUING IN FULL-TIME STUDY

Some of you may be considering continuing straight on with further full-time study. This is a necessary requirement for some professions such as law, while for others it may a deliberate choice. If you are contemplating a career in academia itself, then the natural progression is to a MPhil leading to a PhD. Continuing in full-time education is a big commitment and needs serious contemplation with regard to career planning. While I would in no way discourage anyone from continuing their studies, make sure your motivation is right and that you are not simply trying to avoid going out to earn a living. There is also something to be gained from taking a year out and getting a wider range of experiences under your belt before continuing.

THE UNIVERSITY LEAVER'S CV

When you leave university, you leave behind you the community that you have been in for the past three years or more, and move on to a new start in the workplace. There is no need to keep in touch with anyone if you don't want to – or you might choose to if you've made good friends. Nobody in your workplace need know anything about who you were or how you went about your life at university because it isn't relevant and you have moved on. Hence you have the opportunity to recreate yourself in a more professional image.

This is important because you do not want to go to job interviews presenting yourself as the 'poor student' or the 'person who is not so good at exams'. You want to present yourself as a success and an opportunity that an organisation wants to grab wholeheartedly and invest in further training. So, how do you go about this?

Constructing a good CV is something that is actually very difficult to do on your own without guidance or a sounding board to talk it through with. Obviously there is the standard detail about who you are, where you live, and what qualifications you have, but what you add beyond that is up to you.

One way of differentiating yourself and drawing out life experiences is to present a list of skills, supported by successes that you've achieved through applying these skills. For example:

- *Teamworking* – member of a team of four which won the University Challenge Cup for problem solving.
- *Self-discipline* – worked part-time at Sainsbury's throughout study period with only two days' absence for sickness in the three years of studying; run 5–6 miles every day as part of marathon training.

By drawing out your strengths and illustrating these with successes, your CV will look different to the average undergraduate CV. Also, you need to edit your CV for every job you apply for. Rearrange the order of the skills to match those listed in the job advert, or add more if the person specification outlines something you hadn't considered including. You need to be able to tell an organisation why you are the best person for a job because if you don't know, they have no chance of working it out.

The best way to construct your CV is to talk through your life with someone who doesn't know you very well because they will be able to note the bits that they think are interesting and differentiate you from everyone else. These are the experiences then that you want to draw out as examples to the skills that you list.

In terms of identifying the skills that you want to demonstrate, get some job descriptions for jobs that you are interested in and see what they list as requirements in the person specifications. You want your list of skills to cover that list as a minimum, but also add some extra ones if you have them. If you are good at giving presentations then add that as a skill; if you have leadership experience then add that as a skill. Don't make anything up though as you are likely to be questioned on it at interview and it is unethical to lie on your CV. Think about your strengths and your weaknesses; how can you change your weaknesses into strengths?

If you are particularly sporty and have achieved well in this field, then add your sports achievements under your section on 'hobbies'. If you're not sporty, have a couple of hobbies that you can talk about that make you sound interesting rather than the run-of-the-mill 'reading, films, and cooking' type answers.

Finally try to offer a range of references for different purposes. You will probably need to include a reference from the university. Check with your course tutor who that should be as there is usually a standard process for allocating referees to students in a university. Offer this person as your 'academic reference'. If you have worked at all while you have been studying, try to get your employer to agree to being an 'employer reference'. Finally, if you happen to know someone of standing in the community, or your parents have a friend who is well respected (usually a professional of some type) you can offer them as a 'personal reference'. This allows the prospective employer to select what sort of reference they want about you. Always check with people beforehand that they are happy to be included as referees.

Your final CV, therefore, should look something like the sample opposite – although do play about with the layout to make it look how you want. There is a lot of debate

CV – TED JONES

Full name: Edward Horris Jones

Address: 22 The Green, Hartley-on-Sea, Humberside HU14 8DH

Telephone No: 07978 642233

e-mail: ted.jones@hotmail.com

Qualifications

Hull University (2006–2009)	BA(Hons) Business Studies (2:1)
Hull 6th Form College (2004–2006)	BTEC National Diploma Business Studies (Merit)
Hull Comprehensive (1998–2004)	GCSEs: English (C); Maths (C); Science (C); Art (B); Geography (B); French (C); Physical Education (B).

Other Achievements

Duke of Edinburgh Gold Award

Represented the UK in the Under 21's Hockey team at a European Championships

First Aid certificate

Work Experience

2006–2009 (part-time)	Shop assistant at Tesco including acting as supervisor
2005–2009 (part-time)	Hockey Coach to local under 14 team

Skills Profile

Supervisory skills	Sole responsibility for team of 8 on night shift shop floor at Tesco during 24 hour opening with no need to call duty manager
Coaching skills	Coach under 14 hockey team to win inter-region cup
Communication skills	Clear oral communication skills needed in supervisory role; written communication skills demonstrated in Duke of Edinburgh award

→

Presentation skills	Top mark of the cohort awarded for presentation in final year of degree
Teamworking skills	Member of the silver medal winning under 21 Hockey team at the European Championships 2004; currently trialling for UK Hockey team; ran Tesco shifts as a teamwork effort in supervisory capacity

Hobbies/Interests

Hockey is both a sport and a hobby, and I have played competitively since the age of 11 and continue to do so currently. In addition to Hockey I enjoy playing other sports including football and swimming. I also enjoy attending live rock music concerts and play the guitar as a means of relaxing.

References

Academic Reference: Tutor

Employer Reference: Tesco

Personal Reference: Captain, UK Hockey Team

about whether or not to put date of birth on. I think it gives the reader a feel for how much to expect someone to have achieved if it is on, so if you feel you have achieved lots, then add it; if not, you may choose to leave it off. It is up to you.

FINDING A JOB

There are various routes you can take to help finding a job, and ideally you want to start looking at some of these before you finish your degree, regardless of whether or not you are thinking of taking a year out.

Organisation milk round

Some large organisations undertake a 'milk round' where they circulate round their choice of universities and look for applications from students in their final year. This is a highly selective process and the organisations think that by doing this they get the 'best graduates'. This isn't necessarily the case as they generally don't include all universities so they are being biased with regard to where they choose to select from, and often the 'best graduates' are concentrating on their studies rather than what they do next. What you can be sure of with this is that they get the 'greediest graduates' as sometimes payments are made pre-qualification to candidates who are recruited as a 'golden hello', or other such deals are put in place. All of these can actually detract from your studying and hence are a game that you can choose to enter into or not. If you try and don't get a job you are likely to suffer a drop in self-esteem which is not what you need prior to your final exams.

Recruitment agencies

Some recruitment agencies take on new graduates for short-term, temporary and full-time vacancies depending on what their clients are looking for. Often recruitment agencies don't differentiate between graduates and non-graduates, but differentiate more on work experience. Hence if you have a good base of work experience through part-time work or a sandwich placement, a recruitment agency may be interested in taking you on their books to find you a job. They can certainly be good for finding you seasonal work, such as Xmas fill-ins, summer sales, and so forth.

Graduate recruitment schemes

Rather than doing the formal milk round, many large organisations are now moving to a system where they simply invite applications from any graduates who feel they meet their specification and go through a standard recruitment process. This is a much fairer system in terms of equality of opportunity as anyone who meets the criteria is eligible to apply, rather than it being restricted to those from certain universities.

Internet

Although I don't know of any cases personally, there are evidently people who get jobs through Second Life, as well as through responding to job adverts on the internet. The internet often offers the most up-to-date listings of vacancies and you can also access the classified pages of most newspapers and magazines online. Monster.co.uk is an internet recruitment website that lists thousands of jobs. You can spend hours looking for job opportunities on the internet so be sure of the sort of thing you are after before you start searching or you could waste an awful lot of time.

Job adverts

Some newspapers specialise in certain areas on certain days. *The Guardian*, for example, publishes Education jobs one day, Society jobs another, Business jobs on yet another, and so forth. If there is a professional institute in your field, they probably publish job adverts in their professional journal so it is always worth seeking that out in the library.

Building on your part-time job

If you have been working part time for a large chain while you have been studying, why not explore the career opportunities with them. The large retail outlets, for example, run fantastic graduate training schemes and offer excellent career paths. You are already a known entity to them with a track record already established with regard to attendance, punctuality, and the standard of your work, so in many ways you could have a head start. This is an opportunity that many people miss as it simply doesn't occur to them.

Personal contacts

Although we live in a world of equal opportunities legislation, it is amazing how many people find out about jobs and opportunities through word of mouth. Let people know that you are in the market for a job – tell your parents to tell their friends, or even their employers, as there may be a job to be had from what is now called 'networking'.

LONGER TERM PLANS

There used to be a time, about 20 years ago, when people had a job for life. That is, once they had got a good job in an organisation, they had the choice of staying with that organisation for the rest of their working career, progressing through the ranks at an appropriate pace and learning and developing as they progressed. Then came the downsizing revolution in the 1980s and 1990s and layers of management were removed from organisations, lots of people were made redundant and there was a big shake-up in the labour market. As a result, the concept of 'managing your CV' came to be, which is basically the idea that as an individual you want to make sure your CV is marketable at all times as you never know when you might need to look for a new job. A consequence of this is that people no longer want to stay with one organisation for too long as they worry that it will make them less attractive to other employers as they might lack, for example, adaptability.

Now organisations are having to fight to keep the people they want to remain in the organisation for the future benefit of the organisation and that is the basic history to the concepts of 'talent management' and 'employer of choice', which are words you might hear when you search company websites. Organisations are now struggling to keep people who are worried that staying too long makes them less employable elsewhere.

You need to think about what it is you want to achieve out of life and when. Do you want to have a dominating career or do you want to have a family life as well? Do you want to be a future director of a large organisation, or are you happy earning enough money to keep you in a comfortable manner? Think about these issues as they will impact on how you manage your career and what you do with the opportunities that are presented to you. Also, once you've started down one path, don't think you're stuck on it. You can always step off. Though it is much easier to step off a high-flying career path than it is to step on if you didn't set out with that intent at the start.

CHAPTER SUMMARY

This chapter has tried to put the experience of any single examination into a larger context of learning in general about exams, and about what happens next. The chapter offers a means by which you can reflect on examinations to draw out the learning from both the areas you performed well in and the areas where performance could be improved. The concept of the reflective practitioner was introduced and is an idea that can be taken forward through the rest of your working life, as is the means of drawing out the learning. The tables offered in this chapter could equally be applied to a project, a team event, an incident or any other experience from which reflective learning could be drawn.

This is the last chapter on exams specifically as the final chapter helps you transfer the learning from exams across to other types of assessment.

BUSINESS GAME

Having convinced the frozen food company that Kenya was not a good idea, they have now asked you to explore Pakistan as a new potential market. Given you nearly lost your job over the Kenya fiasco, you don't want to make the same mistake with Pakistan. How can you go about reflecting on the learning from Kenya to ensure you don't make the same mistakes with Pakistan?

This is where you need to go back and think about the areas where you performed well and where there was room for improvement, even if all the improvement you can come up with is to raise warning signals earlier that the country is unlikely to be fruitful for you. Once you've drawn out the learning by reflecting-on-action, start the Pakistan project but keep reflecting-in-action on the process as you go along.

Reference

Schon, D. (1983) *The Reflective Practitioner.* New York: Basic Books.

11 PASSING OTHER ASSESSMENTS

This chapter helps you take all the learning from the previous chapters on examinations and apply that to other forms of assessments. Although there is less time pressure with other forms of assessments, many of the reasons for failure are similar to those of exams, and hence the same learning applies.

This chapter will cover:

- How to plan to pass assessments
- Using all of your learning to pass an assessment
- How to prepare for different types of assessment

USING THIS CHAPTER

INTRODUCTION

This chapter draws out the learning from passing exams and applies it to other forms of assessment such as written assignments and presentations. It demonstrates that the techniques used for passing exams can apply to more than one context and hence being good at exams can also lead to better performance in other forms of assessment. You've already seen how the skills developed in the book can be applied in a business context through the 'business game' at the end of each chapter. Being able to transfer learning and apply it in more than one context is a skill in itself, and of great value in life.

COMMON LESSONS FOR ALL ASSESSMENTS

Regardless of the type of assessment, the points below apply – perhaps more to some forms of assessment than others – but they are still applicable to all. This is because the principles of assessment are the same regardless of the form of assessment chosen. You are being assessed to ensure you have met the learning outcomes and the learning outcomes will have been written in such a way as to fulfil the philosophy and purpose of the university outlined in Chapter 1. That is, the learning outcomes will be designed to develop you as a critical, independent, disciplined thinker who takes a rigorous approach to problem solving, considering the evidence you have been able to find.

HAVE AN ARGUMENT (CHAPTER 1)

The best way to demonstrate to your tutors or any assessor that you really understand something is to argue the case for and/or against it using a range of evidence and sources. This demonstrates that you have firstly read around the subject area and considered the evidence. Secondly, that you understand the evidence well enough to appreciate what is supporting your thinking and what is contrary to it. Thirdly that you are able to articulate why the evidence that is contrary to your view could be interpreted differently or why it can be discounted, and finally, that you are able to weigh up the evidence and draw a conclusion based on your considered judgement.

It really is important to have an argument. Otherwise you are simply presenting what you have read and found out and without telling anyone anything about it. By having an argument you are giving the evidence some meaning, some interpretation and using it to support your views. It is good to have an opinion, it just needs to be supported by evidence so that you can argue it as fact.

The difference between opinion and fact is also an important distinction that needs making. Your opinion is 'I think this' and you may or may not support that with 'because in my experience ...' or some other ending to the sentence. It is good to have an opinion, but your opinion needs to be supported by facts. A fact is when you can say 'I know this because this evidence says ...'. Hence you can be sure that what you are saying is correct because it has been proven and peer reviewed as acceptable. That does not mean that you cannot change your mind at a later point in time. As you come across more evidence, or new evidence emerges at a later date, you may wish to change your opinion because new facts have come to light. What you should not do, and will be penalised very heavily for doing should you do it, is state your opinion as fact when it is unsubstantiated.

USE A MODEL (CHAPTER 1)

Models give us good frameworks against which we can analyse facts, compare and contrast situations, reflect on our personal experiences, or even just start a discussion. Remember that a model is someone else's representation of their data – it is how they have diagrammatically chosen to represent what they found out.

It is good to use a model in an assessment because you can demonstrate that you understand how to use and interpret data, and that you can use one person's ideas (i.e. the model) to discuss another person's ideas (i.e. the other reading that you have undertaken). For example, if you were to present X's model of 'flexible working' which let's say has four segments to it, you could then analyse the rest of your reading in terms of how the other author's ideas fit into the four segments presented by X. This automatically gives you a structure.

When you get to the point in your studies that you are doing your dissertation (if you need to do one), then you will be collecting data for yourself to test out an idea of your own. You may find that the data can be analysed in such a way that you can develop a model of your own, and this is great – but don't worry if it doesn't; it is not compulsory. The important thing is that you are not afraid of using models. Remember, they are someone else's laundry!

SEARCH THE LITERATURE (CHAPTER 2)

A good assessment demonstrates to the marker that you have searched for the answer beyond the obvious places. Your module is likely to have a core textbook which is a good starting point, but academics want to see that you've gone beyond that. While the course reading list is a good place to start, it is not the place to end. Do some searches in the learning resource centre using the electronic databases and try to find something that is relevant to the question you are answering but not mainstream in terms of everyone using it in their assignments. As academics we love it if you use a reference that we haven't included in the reading list – it might even be new to us, which is even better as you are introducing new literature to us and we can then go and read it.

Make use of the electronic resources available to you as they will do a large part of the work for you. Gone are the days when you physically have to leaf through journal contents pages to try to find something relevant. Now search engines do that for you. Try also to use more than one search term to see how that alters the selection of materials drawn to your attention. Remember that the purpose of searching the literature is to find out what is already known about your subject area, so you should look at it as a quest, not as a chore.

READ WIDELY (CHAPTER 2)

Don't just limit yourself to the material that is recommended in the course handbook – read more widely than this. Include newspaper articles on examples that illustrate the topic, or newspaper columns that discuss the issue in the current context. For example, you often find articles in the broadsheets that discuss the state of the economy which could be used as supporting evidence for an economic argument or a business argument. There is often comment in the papers about issues relating to diversity, be it racism, sexism or ageism. These can be used as evidence in a diversity assignment, if only as evidence of what is currently topical.

Have a look also at government websites and statistics such as those published by Her Majesty's Stationery Office (HMSO), the National Audit Office (NAO), the Office of Public Sector Information (OPSI), or any other government website that offers you a range of data and information for free. Often you can find statistical evidence here to support an argument that you are making, without even realising that that information is collected.

KEEP REFERENCES AS YOU GO ALONG (CHAPTER 2)

Remember while you are searching to record all your reading in a database such as EndNote so that you can use the same reference again at a future date for a different purpose. Good assessments are supported by a range of literature and while there is no magic number, it is pleasing to see at least 10 good references in a 3,000 word undergraduate assignment.

Also, make sure that you update the list of references at the end of your assignment as you make reference to the reading in the body of the assignment itself. Failure to do this will result in the reading not being recognised, and it is almost a form of plagiarism by error. You may even fail the assessment if you do not include a reference list. Do it as you go along – just scroll to the end of the document you are writing and enter the bibliographical details – otherwise you have to go back and do it at the end and that is much more time-consuming and stressful because there is always one you can't find!

BE DISCIPLINED WITH YOUR TIME
(CHAPTER 3)

If you are aiming for let's say 10 good references per assignment, you need to do quite a lot of reading as some things you read will turn out not to be relevant to your assignment. It is particularly important that you record those ones on EndNote or your database, as they are likely to be relevant to something you do later on in your studies, so don't waste the fact that you have read them.

Building reading time into your week is important as reading does take time, and it is not something that you can generally do too much of at any one time. By this I mean it is very difficult to spend a whole weekend reading – it is much easier to read one article a day, especially if you can get them down to less than an hour per article.

It is very easy to waste time when you are a student as you are constantly balancing your studies with earning a bit of a living, your family and friends with your independence, getting to grips with living on your own if you've moved out of home – or getting to grips with changing your routine within a household routine that hasn't changed if you are still living at home, as well as getting to grips with a study timetable which has more time 'off' than in lessons. Those that survive and do well are those that develop self-discipline, and that is one of the key skills that university is about.

FIT ASSIGNMENTS INTO YOUR SCHEDULE
(CHAPTER 3)

The most common complaint made by students to course tutors is that all the assignments need to be handed in during the same week. In the same way that you have to learn self-discipline about your use of time, you need to learn discipline with regard to completing assignments. Don't leave them all to the week before they are due in. There is no way you can do four assignments well in one week. Build them into your schedule throughout the semester so that you only have to do the finishing touches the week before they are due in.

The reason why assignments are due in at a similar time is that the tutors like to give you as long as possible in order to complete your assignment, and you might not cover all elements to be included in the assignment until about half way through. This does not mean, however, that you can't get going on them sooner, and indeed you can even submit them early if you really want to.

The important thing is that you start thinking about them early, reading for them early, and drafting what your content is going to be. If you have a good sound plan with the evidence ready, then actually writing the assignment is easy. It is a bit like having your fishbone ready so all you have to do is engage the hand.

SPEND TIME BUILDING THE GROUP WITH GROUPWORK ASSIGNMENTS (CHAPTER 4)

When you are set assignments that need to be completed in a group, establishing the group and how you work together is more important that you probably imagine. If you self-select then you will probably pick friends and one or two 'outsiders' to make up the numbers. This gives an imbalance to the group in that you have already decided that you like your 'friends' so the outsiders are at a disadvantage. This tends to leave the outsiders slightly on the fringe and makes it more difficult for them to contribute fully to the group. The group will be likely to achieve the task but as a series of delegated tasks rather than a cohesive group. Hence it is important that you spend some time as a group getting to know each other so that you can behave as a team rather than a number of people doing interrelated tasks. The results will show in your overall mark.

If you are put into groups with people you don't normally work with then everyone is in the same position and nobody knows anyone, or how they work, or what their preferences are. Now you have to get to know each other first as otherwise you are likely to allocate the wrong tasks to the wrong people. Spending time together like this should also help you learn about yourself. Take the time to reflect on how you are reacting to people and why that might be. What are your prejudices? We all have them – it is how we compensate for them that makes the difference.

FOCUS ON TEAM ROLE STRENGTHS AND ALLOW FOR WEAKNESSES (CHAPTER 4)

When you are put into a group to work together it is very easy to focus on what annoys you about people, or what they are not doing well in the group. This happens in particular when you haven't spent the time getting to know each other well enough at the start of the process, so you are working to your weaknesses rather than your strengths. For example, you'll be getting cross with the person who doesn't really make a contribution – and yet they are probably fulfilling the monitor evaluator role or the completer finisher role. If you recognise that at the outset, after each heated discussion you have, you can turn to your monitor evaluator and ask them what they think, because it is not in their nature to interrupt the discussion with their opinion. Equally, the completer finisher will be worth their weight in gold at the end of the assignment when it comes to writing up the assignment and making sure that everything is ready on time – and although they might nag you, they will make sure it is in on time and to a good standard.

If the group process is going wrong then take some time out as a group, go back to the getting to know you bit, and work out what your strengths and weaknesses are. You could even have a discussion about what you are finding difficult about working with the group so that everyone's views are shared. Other people might be finding your behaviour is leading them to react in the way that you dislike and actually you also need to modify your behaviour.

LOOK FOR SUPPORT WHEN YOU NEED IT (CHAPTER 5)

One reason that group work might not be going well is because members of the group, including yourself, are likely to be feeling stressed about all sorts of things that are going on, and working in the group is seen as yet another stressor. If this is the case, or you feel you are getting to a point where you are too stressed, go and seek some support. You are not alone – the support services exist because the majority of students get to this point.

So how do you know when you need to seek support? If you find yourself crying and you don't know why then your stress level is too high and the stress is literally pouring down your face. If you can't face getting up in the morning and going in to university because of the noise/people/whatever – that feeling of not being able to cope with the environment is a signal that your stress level is too high, because you can't face the added stress of the environment. If you find yourself doing things that add to the problem – for example drinking more when you're depressed; not being able to sleep when you're exhausted; eating too much or too little; spending money on frivolities when you're up to your limit in debt – it's time to go for some support.

Seeking support when you need it as a student is not a sign of weakness, it is quite the opposite. Seeking support demonstrates that you have the strength to find a way out of your difficulties. Asking for help, whether it is from a tutor, a peer, or a counsellor, is the first step to getting over the difficulties you are experiencing. Most students will suffer from study depression at some point during their course, not all will recover from it sufficiently for it not to impact on their overall performance. Don't be one of those students – seek support when you need it.

There is one student experience that I remember very clearly and will share with you here to illustrate the importance of asking for help. In her final year, this student got serious study depression and wasn't coping with the pressure that she was putting herself under to get a good degree. She put so much effort into her assignments and became so obsessed with her grades that she completely threw time management out and didn't progress with her dissertation. As a result, she didn't have a good dissertation completed, but the fear of failure was too much for her to cope with so she plagiarised a previous student's work and submitted that as her dissertation. As one of the markers, I was surprised at the piece of work as it didn't really seem to fit with the student so the second marker and I decided to viva the student. At the viva, she couldn't defend the work because it clearly wasn't hers. She completely broke down as the enormity of what she had done hit her. Now there was the possibility that not only was she failing the dissertation but she could fail her whole degree. My colleague and I got the whole story from her about how much she was struggling, the obsessive behaviour that had resulted and at the end of the hour the student was completely broken and my colleague and I felt absolutely terrible. We were so worried, we walked the student down to the counselling service, and after checking with them later, they called her parents to come and pick her up. We had no option but to fail the dissertation and report it as an academic offence – these situations are out of our hands. We did of course write a report to endeavour to get a more lenient outcome for her as she clearly hadn't set out to cheat – she just hadn't been able to cope and hadn't gone for any support. The outcome was that she had to do another dissertation which could only be awarded a basic pass mark regardless of how good it might be – as is the case when a student fails. She also had the marks wiped out for her assignments in her last semester and had to redo those as well as if they were fails. The 'leniency' was that she did not have to repeat the whole year which is usual in cases of final year plagiarism. My colleague and I never expected to see or hear from her again. We thought she would leave and take a diploma qualification instead of the degree. However, we were wrong. Full credit to the student – she got some support and somehow found the strength to come back and resubmit her final semester's work including a new dissertation, knowing that she would only be able to achieve a third class degree, and submitted first class work all round.

I have never forgotten this student as she is one of the people that I consider to be a 'hero' in my life. She had got so low that there seemed no way out. She then made a very bad decision on how to get out of it and got caught. The consequences were even worse than where she started and she had thrown away everything that she was trying to achieve with no chance now of ever getting there. And yet she sought the support, found the inner strength, and came back to finish so that she could recover as much as possible from her time at university. I'm not sure that I would have been able to do that. I share this story with you to illustrate how getting the right support at the right time can make a difference. If my student in the story had gone for support earlier she wouldn't have chosen to submit a plagiarised piece of work and she would have got a better class of degree than the third she ended up with. I cannot stress enough the importance of going for help when you need it because you don't make good decisions when you are in a low point.

FOCUS ON THE LIGHT AT THE END OF THE TUNNEL (CHAPTER 5)

In Chapter 1 you were asked why you came to university and what you were going to take as your measures of quality. If you find yourself getting to a point where you are really not enjoying your studies and are wondering why you started, go back and revisit those reasons. Focus on the light at the end of the tunnel. This is your university degree course – it is not the rest of your life, although it could impact on the rest of your life depending on your results.

If need be, consider it a three-year sentence which you have to serve as a means of probation into the workplace. It is great if you enjoy your time at university but if you don't, you are definitely not alone. Focus on each semester and module, one at a time, and keep your eye on the end point. With each assessment, focus on what you have to do, and do it. Then it's done; over; move on.

DO WHAT THE QUESTION ASKS (CHAPTER 6)

The most common reason that people fail exams is that they don't answer the question set – a similar thing can happen with other assessments. One sure way of failing an assignment is not doing what you've been asked to do. If you're asked to write a report, don't write an essay!

There is nothing more frustrating as an assessor than people not doing what they've been asked to do, because it doesn't matter how much they demonstrate the requisite knowledge and skill, if they don't meet the marking criteria, they will fail.

To ensure this doesn't happen in an exam, you are advised to write out the question/title. The same holds true here for an assignment. Write out what it is you have to do so that you make sure you do it. If you need to give four examples, give four examples. If you need to use a certain model to illustrate your answer then use that model to illustrate your answer. Simple really – just do what the question asks.

GIVE GOOD EXAMPLES (CHAPTER 6)

In any assessment, you should try to give good examples, particularly current good examples. If you've got to give a presentation, listen to the *Today* programme on Radio 4 on your way into university and you'll probably find there is a relevant discussion that you can use as an example in your presentation.

Watch the news or read a newspaper in the week leading up to an assessment so that you can draw in a highly topical example which demonstrates that you can apply the theory and learning that you are gaining on the module across different domains.

BELIEVE IN YOUR ABILITY TO DO A GOOD ASSIGNMENT (CHAPTER 7)

The more negative you feel about an assessment, the worse your mark is going to be. If you go into a laboratory test thinking that you don't know anything and that everything is going to go wrong then the chances are that it will. If you go in thinking 'I can do this' and keep reminding yourself of that, then the chances are that you will – and if you don't, you'll be able to articulate why you didn't in such a way that the assessors will appreciate that you do still know what you are talking about.

Self-efficacy is very important in assessment situations – particularly when it is a one-off performance such as a lab test, presentation or exam, rather than an assignment that you have plenty of time to prepare for. If you really do believe that you can do something there is much more chance of you succeeding in doing it than if you are questioning your ability.

DRESS TO IMPRESS – IT IS ABOUT PRESENTING (CHAPTER 7)

This is particularly the case for presentations, although lab work does also have dress codes and requirements. Most people fear giving presentations. One way to help deal with the fear is to think of it as an 'acting' exercise. You are going to pretend to be 'Ms X' giving a presentation, and Ms X is a skilled presenter who regularly speaks to public audiences on the topic you are addressing. Hence you don't have think about what you are going to say, you just have to think 'what would Ms X say?'

What you decide to wear also makes an impact. If you go in and present yourself as a professional, you are likely to be treated as a professional; if you go in looking like a shabby student, you are likely to command the respect afforded to a shabby student, no matter how good your content is. A smart, tidy appearance at a presentation is a must – after all, it is about presenting yourself.

Sometimes, little things here can make a big difference. Height of heel, for example, can make you feel different about yourself; or whether you wear a shoe or an ankle boot under trousers. Men really ought to try to wear suits, or at least a smart pair of trousers and a jacket, while women have more flexibility but it should be an outfit that you would wear to an office rather than one for a night out on the town. Shirts and ties add gravitas to men and it also demonstrates to the assessors that you are taking the occasion seriously, and have given some thought and put some effort into your appearance. This also puts the assessors into a positive frame of mind, so their initial perception is 'this is going to be good' rather than 'what have we here?'

The final point about appearance is that you don't want your appearance to detract from the content. If you haven't made an effort to look smart and presentable, assessors are going to be looking at what you are wearing rather than concentrating on what you are saying. Your body posture is likely to be more slumped and relaxed rather than assertive, and your message is likely to get lost in the poor performance when the content might actually have been good.

KNOW YOUR SUBJECT AREA (CHAPTER 8)

The whole purpose of assessment is to test your knowledge and skill. If you haven't bothered to gain the knowledge and/or skill, you are not going to pass, no matter how good you are at blagging. Assessments at university are marked against set criteria so even if you are the most charming presenter who can spin a great story and keep the audience both amused and engaged, if the knowledge content is not there, you will not pass.

The same is true for lab work. If an experiment goes wrong due to circumstances, bad luck or your making a mistake, it is recoverable if you can say 'I've made a mistake here – I've done X and I should have done Y. I did X because I was thinking along this line, and I realise now that I should have been thinking down this other line which would have led me to Y. I can recover this situation by doing Z/I need to start again/How would you like me to proceed?'

You are not expected to be the world's expert on something but you are expected to have done your homework and know your area. You are allowed to make mistakes, but you also need to recognise that you've done that and know both why you made the mistake and how you can correct it, as well as what the correct outcome/answer should be.

Finally, if you do make a mistake, realise it, but if you don't know what to do next, then admit it. Admit to acknowledging the mistake. Explain where you went wrong and why. State that you don't know what you should have done differently but you'll go and look it up.

PRACTICE MAKES PERFECT (CHAPTER 8)

The first time you sit behind the wheel of a car you are likely to stall it rather than pull away perfectly. The first time you try water skiing you are likely to fly over the skis and go face first into the water. It takes practice to learn how to stand up on water skis or how to drive. Why then should this be any different for assessments? Often students think they will be able to do a perfect assessment without any real preparation or practice – why? There are very few things in life that get worse the more times we do them – performance in most activities improves with practice.

Whether it is exam technique under pressure, presenting, lab experiments or a multiple choice test, your performance will improve if you practise. Bore your family or housemates with your presentation every night for the week before you give it; lock yourself away and practise answering multiple choice questions; stay late at the labs so that you can practise your experiment after classes have finished and the equipment becomes available. It really doesn't matter when or where you do it, but you must practise in order to improve your technique, and the better your technique, the better your performance, and the better the grade that you will score.

DIVISION OF LABOUR (CHAPTER 9)

In exams it is important that you separate your brain from your hand so that you don't go off at a tangent. This is also true for lab work. Think about what you are going to do first and then do it. Don't do the two together as you're more likely to go wrong.

With presentations the difficulty comes when you get asked questions at the end. Here again you need to divide labour and separate your brain from your mouth. Nobody expects an instant answer in a presentation. Think about the question – repeat the question if you are unsure of it. Stop, think, decide what to say and then say it. Then stop talking again.

Students go wrong in presentations when they don't answer the questions being asked of them. They hear the question and start answering immediately without stopping to think about what it is that they need to say, and then they keep talking endlessly going round in circles without ever actually answering the question being asked. This may suffice in presentations that you give in the workplace, but it is not okay for an assessment. You must answer the question asked, so make sure that you know what your answer is before you start saying it.

PLAN YOUR ANSWER (CHAPTER 9)

Planning your answer in this respect is important in an assignment as it ensures you include everything you need to, and it is vital in exams to keep you on track. You can use the fishbone technique outlined for the exam for planning an assignment also, or you can do a more detailed plan or mind map. There is no one best way of planning an assignment, it is whatever works best for you – the important thing is that you do a plan.

There are a number of reasons why planning helps improve your assignment. Firstly, you can add to a plan over time, so you can start your plan in week 1 and collect data and evidence and then review the plan in week 3, add more elements, and then go and read some more and so on. You aren't trying to remember everything that should go in it in one session, but rather building the assignment as your knowledge base grows.

Secondly, a plan lets you see an overview of the structure so that you can reflect on the order in which you wish to make points and develop your line of argument. It also gives some direction to your reading and can act as a reminder as to what to include where in the final written assignment.

Finally, when the panic is on and you have four assignments to hand in next week, a good plan makes the writing easy and prevents you from writing the same assignment four times. It also ensures that you answer the question asked.

LEARN FROM THE FEEDBACK YOU GET (CHAPTER 10)

The one thing that has always puzzled me as an academic is students that don't read the feedback we put on their assignments. This was a complete revelation to me a couple of years ago when some students in a focus group let on that they never read their feedback. Why not? They'd moved on to something else; couldn't be bothered to try to decipher the handwriting; the mark told them all they needed to know; and other similarly poor excuses.

If you want to do well at university read the feedback. We don't go through your assignments making comments and notes for fun; we do it to help you learn. The feedback on an assignment should indicate which bits are good and where there is room for improvement. It allows you to go back over your work and reflect on where you performed well and where you need to change your approach. If you don't look at the feedback, how do you know what to change and improve?

DEVELOP YOUR SKILLS AS A REFLECTIVE PRACTITIONER (CHAPTER 10)

Finally, no matter what form of assessment you are undertaking, you want to try to develop your skills and ability to operate as a reflective practitioner. This means that not only are you aware of what you have done in the past and how this could be improved; but you are aware of what you are doing in the present, and can change it if you feel it could be improved as you are doing it.

Reflective practice is not always about the past; it is also about the present. It is about drawing on previous learning and experience and changing what you are doing now and in the future in light of that reflective knowledge.

Whether you are in a lab, giving a presentation or writing yet another assignment, you should be able to improve your performance by drawing on the knowledge and experience of the last time you were in a similar situation, how it felt, how well you did, and what you learnt not to do again.

CHAPTER SUMMARY

This chapter endeavours to be an example of reflective practice at work. It draws on the knowledge and experience set out in all the previous chapters with regard to passing exams, and then adapts it to make it relevant to other forms of assessment.

Hopefully this demonstrates to you that there is more to passing university assessments than luck. It is about hard work, self-discipline, rigour, learning, commitment and the development of technique. This book has been written to help those students who have all of the former but lacked the technique. By setting out the rules of the game and how to play by them, this book aims to help you do better in your assessments by breaking down some of the myths about university, and helping you through the transition from what is required in school work to what is required at university. Hopefully you are now armed with the tools of the trade and every trick and technique you need to succeed. Good luck.

ANNOTATED INDEX

Chapter 3

Chapter 6

Chapter 7

Chapter 11